SOME MORAL
AND
RELIGIOUS TEACHINGS
OF
AL-GHAZZALI

SOME MORAL AND RELIGIOUS TEACHINGS OF AL-GHAZZALI

By

SYED NAWAB ALI, M.A.

State Pensioner, Junagadh
Ex-Fellow University of Bombay
Author of Sirat-i-Rasulullah,
Tarikh-i-Sohof and Qasasul-Haq, etc.

KITAB BHAVAN
New Delhi-110002

KITAB BHAVAN
Exporters & Importers
1784, Kalan Mahal, Daryaganj
New Delhi-110002 (India)
Phones : 3274686, 3263383
Telex : 31-63106 ALI IN

ISBN 81-7151-086-8

First Edition.................... 1988
Second Edition 1991
Third Edition.................. 1994

Published by:
Nusrat Ali Nasri for Kitab Bhavan
1784, Kalan Mahal, Daryaganj
New Delhi-110002 (India)

Printed in India at:
F.M. Offset Printers
Kalan Mahal, Darya Ganj
New Delhi - 110 002 [India]

PREFACE TO THE SECOND EDITION

At the request of Shaikh Muhammad Ashraf of Lahore who is doing good work by publishing works on Islamic Literature in English, I have revised and enlarged my book entitled " Some Religious and Moral Teachings of Al-Ghazzali " which was first published in 1920 by my colleague Alban G. Widgery, M.A., Professor of the Comparative Study of Religions at Baroda College. Below I give a short biographical sketch of Al-Ghazzali and at the end of the book an illuminating extract from his *Minhajul-Abidin's* Prologue under the heading, " The Seven Valleys." It is expected that the book in its present form will prove more useful and instructive.

A short biographical sketch of Al-Ghazzali.

Abu-Hamid Mohammad Ibn Muhammad Al-Ghazzali *Hujjatul-Islam* (the proof of Islam) was born at Tus in A.H. 450 (A.D. 1058). He received his education at Naishapur under Imam-ul-Haramain Juwaini who was a leader of the

Asharite School of thought. During his studies he freely mixed with the leaders of the various sects in Islam and tried to grasp their respective view-points. This spirit of free inquiry and broadmindedness coupled with his great intellectual powers and genuine search after Truth made him one of the most original thinkers that Islam has produced. In A.H. 478 after the death of his teacher, he left Naishapur and went to the court of Nizamul-Mulk the great vizier of the Saljuks who attached him to his retinue of theologians until A.H. 484 when he was appointed professor in the Nizamia College at Baghdad. For four years he taught and wrote *Fiqh* (Canon law) and also controversial books against the Batinias and other heretical sects. A critical study of Greek philosophy and its depressing effect on *Iman* (Faith) dissatisfied him with intellectualism. Philosophy had now no charms. theology as taught in those days appeared as a dead letter and all seemed blank to him. He would have taken refuge in Sufiism but he knew that true Sufiism was حال (ecstatic state of mind) and not قال (tall talk). A graphic account of this inward struggle is given by Al-Ghazzali himself in his *Al Munqid min ad Dalal* which he wrote five years before his death. At last unable to bear the mental shock any more he put behind him his brilliant position and worldly honour and fled, so to say, from Baghdad in A.H. 488. Then he made a pilgrimage to Mecca, visited Medina, Jerusalem and other holy places. Praying by the side of Abraham's tomb at Hebron he took a vow not to indulge in disputations, not to attend 'Darbars' and not to accept any stipend. The following anecdote will give an idea of how he was purifying his soul. In one of his wanderings while reading "books in running brooks and sermons in stones" he halted at a mosque where from the pulpit he heard the preacher saying, "So says our Imam Ghazzali." Said Gazzali to himself, "How pleasing is this remark to thee, O my conceited self, but I would not tolerate the enjoyment of the pleasure any more. Leave this place at once and go where nobody talks of thee." From such strugglings after Truth and purity of heart did Ghazzali win to a bright faith, a sure conviction and a power of leading others to that *Sirat-e-Mustaqeem* (the Straight Path) which was revealed in the Quran. He now felt it his sacred duty to bequeath to posterity what he had gained, not through speculative methods but by ecstatic experience. Political conditions of those times gave also a stimulus to his resolve. The march of the Crusaders from Christendom and the fall of Jerusalem in A.H. 492—where in the Great Mosque deplorable scenes which disgraced the conquest of Titus in 70 A.D. were renewed—was a national calamity. And the discord among the Muslim princes and the weakness of the Fatimite Khalif Mustaali in Egypt enabled the Franks to establish themselves in the countries of Islam. Ghazzali had to leave Palestine ; he went to Egypt but soon returned from Alexandria.

During seven years of retreat in different places with periods of return to his family from time to time, he composed his great work *Ihya Ulum-id-Din* which immortalised his name and earned for him the illustrious title of *Imam Hujjatul-Islam*. In A.H. 499 he was forced by the Saljuk Sultan to teach in the Nizamia College at Naishapur, but he resigned after a short period and retured to his native place in Tus where he died in peace on the 14th of Jamadi-us-sani A.H. 505 (December 19, 1111).

In his *Literary History of Persia*, vol. I, p. 293, Browne has quoted Tholuck thus :—

"Ghazzali," says he, "if ever any man has deserved the name, was truly a divine, and he may justly be placed on a level which Origen, so remarkable was he for learning and ingenuity, and gifted with such a rare faculty for the skilful and worthy exposition of doctrines."

Ghazzali's influence on Eurpean thought, even the most modern, has been marked. In the Middle Ages it flowed through the *pugio fidei* of Ramon Marti, and affected first Thomas Aquinas and later Pascal.

LUCKNOW

NAWAB ALI

1st May, 1944

CONTENTS

INTRODUCTION

By Alban G. Widgery M.A.
Professor of the Comparative Study of Religion
The College, Baroda.

THE Comparative Study of Religion, interesting as a form of intellectual research, has for many a further value in the influence it may exert upon the widening and the deepening of the religious life. The practical value may become more and more acknowledged if, as signs suggest, the reality of the religious experience is more keenly felt and mankind recognise the place of religious goods in the highest type of life. Though it is certainly premature to say that there is much serious acknowledgment and recognition of these values amongst the peoples of the world, there are reasons to think that tendencies of thought and feeling in this direction are increasing in power. One of the best means of aiding the Comparative Study of Religions and promoting these tendencies is by the publication of important books connected with the religions, representing the views of leading thinkers and saints.

If we turn to Islam, we find that some Western writers describe it as in a condition of progressive decay, while others would have us believe that its onward march is a menace. It is well to be able to avoid the obvious purpose which lies behind both contentions. Nevertheless, to the present writer it appears true to say that there is much stagnation in Islam—(in which religion is there not ?)—and that its spirit is often lost and its real teachings neglected owing to the general use of Arabic in the recitation of the Quran by persons entirely ignorant of that language, and also to the prevalent mechanical conception of the character of the Quran as a form of divine revelation. We believe that the Comparative Study of Religions will help to turn the attention of Muslims away from these to the emphasising of the essential spirit of Islam. This should be central and normative in the rising movements of reform and rejuvenescence. In this connection, as bringing out this spirit, it is especially appropriate, both for the students of the religions and for those directly interested in the spiritual revival in Islam, to publish in an easily accessible form some of the religious and moral teachings of Ghazzali. A Western scholar has written of him that he is " the greatest, certainly the most sympathetic figure in the history of Islam......the only teacher of the after generations ever put by Muslims on a level with the four great Imams."[1] And he goes on to remark further : " In the renaissance of Islam which is now rising to view, his time will come and the new life will proceed from a renewed study of his works."[2] But Dieterici says of him : " As a despairing sceptic he springs suicidally into the all-God (*i.e.* all-pervading deity of the Pantheists) to kill all scientific reflection."[3] To justify such a judgment would indeed be impossible if the whole course of Ghazzali's works is taken into consideration. The greatest eulogy is perhaps that of Tholuck : " All that is good, worthy, and sublime, which his great soul had compassed, he

---

1. D. B. Macdonald : *Muslim Theology*, London, 1903, p. 215. This book gives the best account of Al Ghazzali's work yet available in English.

2. ibid. p. 240.

3. Quoted in E. G. Browne : *Literary History of Persia*, 1903. Vol. I. p. 294.

bestowed upon Muhammedanism, and he adorned the doctrines of the Quran with so much piety and learning that in the form given them by him, they seem, in my opinion, worthy of the assent of Christians. Whatsoever was most excellent in the philosophy of Aristotle or in the Sufi mysticism, he discreetly adapted to the Muhammedan theology. From every school he sought the means of shedding light and honour upon religion, while his sincere piety and lofty conscientiousness imparted to all his writings a sacred majesty."[1]

One feature of Ghazzali's attitude has considerable significance in looking to an increased study of his works as a factor towards the revivification of Islam : his tolerance. Although regarding Al Hallaj's expressions, (for example, I am the truth, *i.e.* God) as incautious, he helped to defend him and to save him from execution on a charge of blasphemy. He wrote a treatise on tolerance : *The Criterion of the Difference between Islam and Heresy*. In this teaching of tolerance he felt himself to be pointing back to the policy of the earliest Muslim times and to the greatest authorities of early

---

1. ibid. p. 293.

Islam. He "strove to attract the souls of his fellow Muslims to spiritual faith which unifies, to worship at the altars which are in the hearts of men."[1]

The influence of Ghazzali has been represented by Mr. Macdonald as chiefly that he led men back from scholastic labours upon theological dogmas to living contact with study and exegesis of the Quran and Traditions ; gave Sufism an assured position within the Church of Islam ; and brought philosophy and philosophical theology within the range of the ordinary mind.[2]

Al Ghazzali has given some account of his own religious development in a work entitled *Munqidh min ad-Dalal*. This account is significant, but as the Baron Carra de Vaux remarks, his eventual explicit adoption of a Sufi mysticism was not merely a consequence of the failure of his other attempts to find a solution to life's profoundest problems but a result of his early influences. For, soon after his birth at Tus in Khorasan in 450 A.H. (1059 A.D.), his father

---

1. I. Goldzieher : *Vorlesungen uber den Islam*. Leipzig, 1910, p. 185. See translation in the 'Indian Philosophical Review' by the present writer : Vol. I. pp. 260-6.

2. Op. cit. pp. 238—40.

died and he was brought up by a Sufi. Nevertheless his mystical leanings did not assert themselves vigorously till he was well on to maturity. Up to that time he devoted himself to the usual studies of canon law, the orthodox theology, the doctrines of the Mutazilites, and a variety of other subjects, including the works of the Sufis. For a time he was a student of the Asharite Imam Al Haramayn at Nysabur. He himself represents his attitude as at this time that of one working and wishing for reputation and wealth. In 484 A.H. he was honoured by appointment to the "University" or "Academy" of Baghdad, where he soon acquired great renown as lawyer and theologian.

On the threshold of maturity he was afflicted by doubts as to the validity and worth of the theological and philosophical bases of his religious beliefs. The strain of his reflection and the intensity of anxiety to reach a secure faith seem to have caused a breakdown of his health. With unexpected suddenness he left Baghdad. That was in 488 A.H. (1095 A.D.) He had examined in all details the traditional orthodox scholastic system of the *Kalám*, the positions of the Mutazilites and the philosophers, and in the light of his new doubts and experiences turned again also to a closer study of the writings of the leading mystics, such as Abu Talib, Al Muhasibi, and Al Junayd. His early training had predisposed him to the acceptance of mysticism, and this acceptance was led up to by the conclusions of his reflection, in which, it has been maintained, he carried doubt as far back as did Descartes.

Thus he himself writes: "A thirst to comprehend the essential nature of all things was, indeed, my idiosyncrasy and distinctive characteristic from the beginning of my career and prime of my life: a natural gift and temperament bestowed on me by God and implanted by Him in my nature by no choice or device of my own, till at length the bond of blind conformity was loosed from me, and the beliefs which I had inherited, were broken away when I was little more than a boy."[1]

Carra dé Vaux[2] thus graphically describes the process in Al Ghazzali's mind, as he himself suggests it to us: "Religious beliefs he reflected are transmitted by the authority of parents; but authority is not proof. To arrive at

1. From *Al Munqidh min ad-Dalal.*
2. *Gazali*, Paris, 1902, pp. 44-45.

certitude it was necessary for him to reconstruct all his knowledge from the very foundation. With a vivid feeling of this necessity, he aspired to certitude, defining it in a purely psychological fashion as a state in which the mind is so bound up with and so satisfied with a piece of knowledge that nothing might henceforth deprive him of it. This curious definition, which is applied to religious faith as well as to scientific knowledge, does not escape from being purely subjective. As one might foresee, the great desire for certitude only led him at first into a series of doubts. As he sought this state of perfect assurance, step by step he saw it recede before him. He looked for certitude in the perceptions of the senses, with the result that he could no longer trust his senses. Sight, the most powerful of the faculties of sense, for example, led him to the perception of an immovable shadow on the sun and an hour afterwards this shadow was gone. Sight showed him a star which is very small, and geometry made him recognise it to be greater than the earth. Then he turned to the first principles of reason ; but the perception of the senses took its revenge in saying to him : 'Previously you believed in me and you abandoned me when this judge reason presented itself. If this judge had remained hidden you would have continued to believe in me. Who can tell you that beyond the reason there is no other judge, which, if it made itself evident, would convict reason of falsehood ?' That is a movement of thought which is dramatic enough, though perhaps a little artificial. The thinker continued his search for the certain. He halted and concerned himself with the famous comparison of life with a dream and death with an awakening. Perhaps after that awakening he would see things in a different manner from that in which he then saw them. Mysticism thus suggested itself to him : This actual dream of death could be anticipated by the condition of ecstasy, by less than ecstasy, by a light which God pours into the heart. In this light, he saw not only the truth of the dogmas of the faith or the beauty of the moral life, but he was assured of the truth of the first priniciples of reason,—the basis of all knowledge and all reasoning. He doubted no longer ; he was cured of his pains ; he had found certitude and peace."

On leaving Baghdad, he retired to meditate in the mosques of Damascus, and is further reported to have made pilgrimages to Jerusalem, Hebron (the burial place of Abraham), Medina and Mecca. In abandonment to his immediate religious experience of the love of God he found more peace. In the course of time he associated again more definitely with his family. Eventually in 499 A.H. (1106 A.D.) he was ordered by the Sultan to teach in the Academy at Nysabur. After a life in which he had written a large number of independent treatises and indeed brought about a great change in the tendencies of Islam, he died at his native town of Tus in 505 (1111 A.D.)

If in his initial process of doubt Ghazzali resembled Descartes, in his view of causality he reminds us of Hume; in his general attitude he approaches Kant and Schleiermacher. On the one hand he insists on the limitation of the efficiency of the theoretical reason, on the other he finds in will, in the moral and the religious experience, a more immediate avenue to real knowledge. For the study of religion in our day it is important to note that Ghazzali (here unlike Kant) sees in religious experience a way to certitude. But in this he is led to acknowledge that the advance of the human mind towards its goal of real knowledge and peace is dependent upon an active influence of God upon man. It may be maintained that he puts here in religious terminology the central idea of the Aristotelian conception of Scholastic times, the relation of the "Active Intelligence" to the minds of men. His view enabled him to give a due position to the Prophet and the Quran. For the knowledge of God is to be conceived as coming not in immediate mystical intuition to all alike, but while in some degree to all, to some in a special degree. These are the prophets. The position which Maimonides presents in his *Guide to the Perplexed*[1] with relation to religious knowledge and the functions of the prophets is parallel with that of Ghazzali.

From the accompanying list and classification of the works of Ghazzali, it will be seen that he was a writer on all sides of the theory

---

1. See the English translation of the Guide by Friedlander: *The Guide to the Perplexed*, London, especially pp. 225 ff. Al Ghazzali's works were so widely studied that it is hardly possible to suppose that Maimonides was not influenced by them. The influence may have been direct, as Maimonides was not only a student in Spain but also physician in the court of Saladin in Alexandria. Indirectly the influence may have come through the Jewish poet Yehuda Halevi.

and practice of his religion. He was an authority on canon law and jurisprudence, and a commentator of the Quran. He examined the positions of the Scholastic theologians, and found that they depended entirely on the acceptance of their initial dogmatic assumptions. The disputes of the Scholastics amongst themselves appeared to have little or no relation with religious life, rather if anything they were a hindrance to true religion. And in face of the philosophers the Scholastic theologians were almost helpless. But the books which exerted the greatest influence both within and beyond Muslim circles, and the books that still retain their interest to-day are the *Maqasid ul Falasafa* (The Aim or Goal of the Philosophers) the *Tahafat ul Falasafa* (the Refutation of the Philosophers) and the *Ihya-al-Ulum-id-Din* (The Renovation of the Sciences of Religion.) In the first of these he gives an account of the different philosophical positions which were more or less prevalent. In the second he critically examines those positions. In the third he gives a general survey with a constructive purpose chiefly moral and religious. It is due to this last work more than all others that Ghazzali has been called " The Regenerator of Religion " : "The Proof of Islam." The *Ihya* " expounds theology and ethics from the moderate Sufi school." Though it was committed to the flames, chiefly in Spain, probably by those holding opinions which Ghazzali had bitterly attacked, it soon established its position in the Muslim world, in which it has been widely studied up to present. From it the passages translated in this book are taken. The following table of contents will show the range of the subjects with which it deals.

THE RENOVATION OF THE SCIENCES OF RELIGION

PART I.

1. On Knowledge. Articles of Faith.
2. On Purification.
3. Prayer and Its Meaning.
4. Zakat and Its Meaning.
5. Fasting and Its Meaning.
6. Pilgrimage and Its Meaning.
7. The Reading of the Quran.
8. Varieties of Orisons.
9. The Order of Praying, and Vigils.

PART II.

PART III.

9. Pride and Vanity.
10. Self-deception.

PART IV.

1. Repentance.
2. Patience and Thanksgiving.
3. Hope and Fear.
4. The Poor and the Hermit.
5. Unity of God, and Dependence on Him.
6. On Love, Ecstasy, and Joyous Submission to His Will.
7. On Intention, Sincerity and Truth.
8. Meditation.
9. Contemplation and taking a Warning.
10. On Death and the After-Life.

Against the philosophers he argued for the belief in the reality of the divine attributes and against the view of the eternity of the world. He contended against the theory that there would be no physical punishments and rewards hereafter, maintaining, as he did, the doctrine of the resurrection of the body. He virtually denied that there is real causal connection in events as experienced by us : but only sequence : in this he adumbrates theory of Hume. For Ghazzali, God is the only efficient cause. From the scepticism to which his consideration of philosophy led him, he turned to the acceptance of revelation, this is found in the mystic experience and in the words of saints and prophets, especially the Prophet Muhammad.

The knowledge of moral principles Ghazzali conceived as coming not through rational reflection but by immediate intuition of the divine character revealing itself. Moral truths come especially through moral and religious teachers as the most fit persons for the transmission of these revelations. He possessed great skill in psychological analysis of moral conditions, and passages in illustration of this have been included here, treating of pride and vanity, friendship and sincerity. As almost all great practical moral and religious teachers, Ghazzali makes considerable use of apt stories, and of striking sayings from the saints and prophets. He continually harks back to the time of the Prophet and his "Companions."

Ghazzali's abandonment of his academic position at Baghdad, his retirement to mosques and journeying on pilgrimage, are sufficient evidence that he recognised that the truth of mysticism could not be tested by theoretical reflection but only by an attempt at practice. Only the experience itself could prove its own reality. He appears to have held that for the attainment of the condition of ecstasy the means of asceticism and meditation should be used. But it does not seem quite correct to suggest as does Carra de Vaux that Ghazzali did not recognise the fact of divine "grace," though he did not use a corresponding term. The beatific vision of the mystic certainly depended in part, for Ghazzali, on God's mercy in removing the veil. How far he himself was successful in attaining the bliss of the mystic vision it is impossible to tell : in this direction he gained no such reputation as did several other Sufis. He taught that repentance, a moral coversion, is a necessary preliminary to the mystic life, and he fought against a common tendency of mystics towards antinomianism. Similarly he tried to avoid the danger of interpreting the union of the soul with God as its identification with God in a pantheistic view of the universe. Goldzieher says he differed from the Sufis generally in the rejection of their pantheistic aims and low estimate of religious ordinances [1]

1. op. cit. p. 179.

A LIST OF WORKS BY AL GHAZZALI*

A—CANON LAW

Title	*Subject*	*Place and date of publication*
K. *Wajiz* (Compendium)	Canon Law.	Cairo. 1317 A.H.
Risalat-ul-Qudsiyya.	(Tanscendence of God) included in *Ihya* as the 3rd section of the 2nd Chapter of its Book 1.	

*This list is taken from *A Chronological List of Muslim Works on Religion and Philosophy* which has been for a short time in preparation at the Seminary for the Comparative Study of Religion, Baroda, by Professor Jamil-ur-Rehman of Hyderabad, and Professor F. S. Gilani of Surat, Fellows of the Seminary. The list has been compared with that of Shibli in his Urdu life of Ghazzali (Cawnpore 1902) whose classification is followed with slight modification.

Anqud ul Mukhtasar	Summary of Jowim's Mukhtasar.	
Ghait ul Ghor fi Masail il Dor.	Divorce.	
Ghaur ul Durar.		
Qanun ul Rasul.	The Canon Law of the Prophet.	
	B—JURISPRUDENCE.	
Al Mustasfa.	Jurisprudence.	Boulac. 1322 A.H.
Al Manhul wal Muntahal.	Doctrines falsely attributed to others and falsely claimed by some. Jurisprudence.	
Wajiz fil Furu.	Jurisprudence.	Egypt. 1305 A.H.

Khulasat ul Fiqh (Quintessence of Jurisprudence).	Jurisprudence		
Al durr ul Manzum fi sirr il Muktum Wasit.	An Exposition of Shafiite Jurisprudence.		
	C—LOGIC.	Cairo.	1328 A.H.
Mizan ul Amal.	Logic.	Cairo.	
Mihakkul Nazar fil Mantaq (Whetstone of reflection)	Logic.		
Mayar ul Ilm.	Logic.		
Al Maarif ul Aqliyyah wal Allahiyyah Al Mutaqid.	Discourses on Logic.		
Mayar ul Ilm fi Fannil Mantaq (The weighing scale of the Science).	On Logic.	Cairo.	1329 A.H.

D—PHILOSOPHY.

Ihya u-Ulum-id-Din.	(The most important book for his philosophy).	Cairo.	1322, 1324	A.H.
		Egypt.	1282	„
		Lucknow.	1281	„
		Meerut.	1280	„
Maqasid ul Falasafa (The aims of the philosophers).		Cairo.	1326	„
Mazmun bihi ala Ghairi Ahlihi.	Exposition of Ghazzali's own views.	„	1328	„
Kitab-ul-Arbain.	Abridgement of *Ihya.*	„	1328	„
Risalat ul Luduniyya	Knowledge (Ilham and Wahi)	„	1328	„
Al-Kashfu-wat-Tabyin fi Ghurur il khalqi Ajmain.	On the delusion of men in general. (On the margin of Ash-Shurain's Tanbihul Mughtarrin.)	„	1324	„

Faysalut-Tafriqa baynal Islam-i-waz-Zandiqah.	Refutation of Atheists.	Cairo. 1325 A.H.
Al Fikratu al Ibrah.	Meditation and Contemplation.	
Tahafat ul Falasafa.	Destruction of the Philosophers.	„ 1321 „
Iljam ul Awam.	Abbreviation of the *Ihya.*	
Al-Imla-u-' an ishkalat-il-Ihya.	Statements on disputed passages of *Ihya.*	In the margin of 1334 edition of *Ihya.*
Mustazhiry.	A guide for novices.	
Al Hikmat-u-fi-Makhluq-i-Ilahi.	Wisdom of God.	Cairo. 1326 A.H.
Hakikat ul Ruh.	On Soul.	

E—ETHICS.

Badayai ul Hidayah.	Ethics.	Cairo. 1317, 1326 A.H.
Kimiya i Saadat.	Ethics.	,,
Tibr ul Masbuk.	An ethical mirror for princes. A letter.	,, 1317 ,,
Ayyuh al Walad.	A letter of faith and conduct.	,, 1328 ,,

F—THEOLOGY : EXEGETICAL AND DOGMATICAL.

Al durr ul Fakhira	On eschatology.	,, 1322 ,,
Yaqul ul Tawil fi Tafsir il Tanzil.	A commentary on the Quran in 40 vols. Not found.	

K. Iqtisad fil-I'tiqad.	Exposition of Faith.	Cairo.	
Fadhaih ul Abahiya.	The exposure of Doctrines of the Freethinkers.		
Al Quistas ul Mastaqim.	(No Imam is necessary except the Prophet himself).	„	
Al Qual ul Jamil fil Raddi ala man Ghayyar al Injil.	Criticism of those who have changed the text of the Bible.		
Haqiqat ul Qualain.	An Exposition of truth of two sayings.		
Tadlis Iblis.	The intrigue of the devil.		
Jawahir ul Quran.	A collection of the selected verses of the Quran.	„	1329 A.H.

4

Risalat ul Wahdah wal-I'tiqad.	A brief letter on preaching and belief.		
Risalat-ul-'Aqaid.	Doctrines of Islam and the duties of rulers.	Cairo.	1325 A.H.
Al Maqasid ul Khilaf fi fan il Kalam.	Different theories of Kalam		

G—SUFIISM.

Al-Adab-fid-Din.	(Fitting behaviour in religion).	„	1328 „
Al-Qawaid-ul-Ashara.	(A very brief summary of general advice on religious matters).	„	1328 „
Maqasid ul Hasana Sharh Asma i-illahi'l Husna.	An exposition of Divine Names.	„	1322 „

Minhaj ul 'Abidin.	The path of the Devout (said to be the last of his works).	Cairo.	1313 A.H.
Nasihat-ul Talmiz.	An Epistle.	,,	1295 ,,
Kitab Asrar al Anwar.			
Madkhal ul Suluk ila Manazil il Muluk.	A Guide for kings.		
Al Munqid min ad Dalal (Deliverer from error).	Autobiographical statement of his spiritual progress.	,,	1303, 1329 A.H.
Tajrid fil-Kalimat il Tauhid.	Exposition of Kalima.	,,	1325 ,,
Murshid ul Talibin.	A Guide for novices.		
Mishkat ul anwar fi Lataif il Akhbar (Niche for the lights).	Esoteric exposition of the verse "God is the light of heavens and earth."	,,	1325 ,,

Kitab ul-Madnun-i-Saghir.	Esoteric exposition of the verse " Then shaped him and breathed of His Spirit into him."	Cairo. 1328 A.H.
Makashifat-ul-Qulub.	(Abridgment of a work of doubtful authorship ascribed to Al Ghazzali).	Boulac & Cairo 1360 A.H. Cairo. 1306 A.H.

Note :—In the 13th century during the Mangol eruption many libraries also were burnt and destroyed by the heathens. Ghazzali's *Tafsir* in 40 vols. was thus lost with some other works. Let it also be noted that a book entitled " Sirr ul alamain," a manual for kings to worldly success, attributed to Ghazzali, is apocryphal.

Nawab Ali.

MORAL AND RELIGIOUS TEACHINGS OF AL GHAZZALI

THE NATURE OF MAN[1]

THOUGH man shares with the other animals external and internal senses, he is at the same time also endowed with two qualities peculiar to himself, knowledge and will. By knowledge is meant the power of generalisation, the conception of abstract ideas, and the possession of intellectual truths. By will is meant that strong desire to acquire an object which after due consideration of its consequences has been pronounced by reason to be good. It is quite different from animal desire, nay, it is often the very opposite of it.

In the beginning children also lack these two qualities. They have passion, anger, and all the external and internal senses, but will finds its expression only later. Knowledge differs according to the capacity for it, according to the latent powers in a man. Hence there is a variety of

1. *Ihya*, iii, 1.

stages amongst Prophets,[1] the Ulama, the Sufis and the Philosophers. Further progress is possible even beyond these stages, for divine knowledge knows no bounds. The highest stage is reached by one to whom all truths and realities are revealed intuitively, who by virtue of his exalted position enjoys direct communion and close relation with the Most Holy. The real nature of this position is known only to him who enjoys it. We verify it by faith. A child has no knowledge of the attainments of an adult ; an adult is not aware of the acquisitions of a learned man. Similarly, a learned man is not cognisant of the holy communion of the saints and the prophets, and of the favours bestowed on them. Although the divine blessings descend freely, those are fit recipients of them whose hearts are pure and wholly devoted to Him. "Verily," says the Hadis, " the desire of the virtuous is to hold communion with me, and I long to look at them." "He who approaches me a span, I approach him an arm."[2] The divine favours are not withheld, but hearts bedimmed by impurity fail to

1. This word is used both for *Rasul* and *Nabi*, but the Muslim notion of *Rasul* differs from that of *Nabi*. Malachi was a prophet (*Nabi*), but Moses was more than a prophet (*Rasul*). Thus in *St. Matthew* XI. 9 we have : " But wherefore went ye out to see a prophet ? Yea, I say unto you, and much more than a prophet."
2. Abuhuraira's report given in *Bokhari* and *Muslim*.

receive them. "Had it not been that the devils hover round the hearts of men, they would have seen the glories of the Kingdom of the Heaven."[1]

The superiority of man consists thus in his being cognisant of divine attributes and actions. Therein lies his perfection; thus he may be worthy of admission to God's Presence.

The body serves as a vehicle for the soul, and the soul is the abode for knowledge which is its fundamental character as well as its ultimate object. The horse and the ass are both beasts of burden, but a superiority of the former is found in its being gracefully adapted for use in battle. If the horse fails in this it is degraded to the rank of mere burden-bearing animals. Similarly with man. In certain qualities man resembles a horse and an ass, but his distinguishing trait is his participation in the nature of the angels, for he holds a middle position between the beast and the angel. Considering the mode of his nourishment and growth he is found to belong to the vegetable world. Considering his power of movement and impulses he is a denizen of the animal kingdom. The distinguishing quality of

---

1. Reported by Abuhuraira in Ahmad's *Musnad* Egypt. 1300 A.H.

knowledge lifts him up to the celestial world. If he fails to develop this quality and to translate it into action he is no better than a grunting pig, a snarling dog, a prowling wolf, or a crafty fox.

If he wishes for true happiness, let him look upon reason as a monarch sitting on the throne of his heart, imagination as its ambassador, memory as treasurer, speech as interpreter, the limbs as clerks, and the senses as spies in the realms of colour, sound, smell, etc. If all these properly discharge the duties allotted to them, if every faculty does that for which it was created—and such service is the real meaning of thanksgiving to God—the ultimate object of this sojourn in this transitory world is realised.

Man's nature is made up of four elements, which produce in him four attributes, namely, the beastly, the brutal, the satanic, and the divine. In man there is something of the pig, the dog, the devil, and the saint. The pig is the appetite which is repulsive not for its form but for its lust and its gluttony. The dog is passion which barks and bites, causing injury to others. The devil is the attribute which instigates these former two, embellishes them and bedims the sight of reason which is the divine attribute.

Divine reason, if properly attended to, would repel the evil by exposing its character. It would properly control appetite and the passions. But when a man fails to obey the dictates of reason, these three other attributes prevail over him and cause his ruin. Such types of men are many. What a pity it is that these who would find fault with those who worship stones do not see that on their part they worship the pig and dog in themselves ! Let them be ashamed of their deplorable condition and leave no stone unturned for the suppression of these evil attributes. The pig of appetite begets shamelessness, lust, slander, and such like ; the dog of passion begets pride, vanity, ridicule, wrath and tyranny. These two, controlled by the satanic power, produce deceit, treachery, perfidy, meanness etc., but if divinity in man is uppermost the qualities of knowledge, wisdom, faith, and truth, etc. will be acquired.

Know then that mind is like a mirror which reflects images. But just as the mirror, the image, and the mode of reflection are three different things, so mind, objects, and the way of knowing are also distinct. There are five reasons which may prevent the object from being reflected in the mirror. 1. There may be something wrong with the mirror. 2. Something other than the mirror may prevent the reflection. 3. The object may not be in front of it. 4. Something may come between the object and the mirror. 5. The position of the object may not be known, so that the mirror may be properly placed. Similarly, for five reasons, the mind fails to receive knowledge. 1. The mind may be imperfect, like the child's. 2. Sin and guilt may bedim the mind and throw a veil over it. 3. The mind may be diverted from the real object. For example, a man may be obedient and good, but instead of rising higher to the acquisition of truth and contemplation of God is contented with bodily devotions and acquirement of means of living. Such a mind, though pure, will not reflect the divine image for his objects of thought are other than this. If this is the condition of such mind, think what will be the state of those minds which are absorbed in the gratification of their inordinate passions. 4. An external screen may, as it were, come before the objects. Sometimes a man who has subjugated his passions still through blind imitation or prejudice fails to know the truth. Such types are found amongst the votaries of the Kalam. Even many virtuous men also fall a prey to it and blindly stick to their dogmas. 5. There may be ignorance of the means for the acquisition of truth. Thus, for illustration, a man wants to see his back in a mirror : if he places the mirror before his eyes he fails to see his back ; if he keeps it facing his back it will still be out of sight. Let him then take another mirror and place one before his eyes and the other facing his back in such a position that the image of the latter is reflected in the former. Thus he will be able to see his back. Similarly the knowledge of the proper means is a key to the knowledge of the unknown from the known.

The divine dispensation is liberal in the distribution of its bounties, but for reasons mentioned above, minds fail to profit by them. For human minds partake of the nature of the divine and the capacity to apprehend truth is innate. The Quran says : " Surely We offered the trust to the heavens and the earth and the mountains, but they declined to bear it up and were afraid of it and man took it up. Surely he is not just (to himself) and is ignorant."[1] In this passage the innate capacity of man is hinted at and refers to the secret power of knowing God, latent in

---

1. *Quran* XXXIII. 72.

human minds by virtue of which they have preference over other objects and the universe. The Prophet says : " Every child is born in the right state (Fitrat) but his parents make him a Jew, a Christian, or a Magian." And again : " Had it not been that evil spirits hover round the hearts of the sons of Adam they would have seen the kingdom of heaven." Ibn Umar reports that the Prophet was once asked as to where God is found, either on earth or in heaven. " He is in the hearts of His faithful servants," replied the Prophet.

It will not be out of place to throw some light here on the following terms which are often vaguely applied while dealing with the question of human nature.

1. Qalb (heart) has two meanings : (*a*) A conical-shaped piece of flesh on the left side of the chest, circulating blood, the source of animal spirits. It is found in all animals. The heart thus belongs to the external world and can be seen with material eyes. (*b*) A mysterious divine substance which is related to the material heart like the relation between the dweller and the house or the artisan and his implements. It alone is sentient and responsible.

2. Ruh (spirit) means (*a*) a vapoury substance which issues from the material heart, and quickens every part of the body. It is like a lamp which is placed in a house and sheds its light on all sides. (*b*) The soul which is expressed in the Quran as "divine commandment"[1] and is used in the same sense as the second meaning of Qalb, mentioned above.

3. Nafs (self) which means (*a*) the substratum for appetite and passion. The Sufis call it the embodiment of vices. (*b*) The ego which receives different names in accordance with the qualities acquired from changes in its conditions. When in subjugating passions it acquires mastery over them and feels undisturbed, it is called the *peaceful self* (Nafsi mutmainna). The Quran says : "Nafs that art at rest. Return to thy Lord well pleased with Him, well pleasing." When it upbraids man for his actions it is called *conscience* (Nafsi lauwama). When it freely indulges in the gratification of his passions, it is called the *inordinate self* (Nafsi ammara).

1. *Quran* XVII. 85.

HUMAN FREEDOM AND RESPONSIBILITY[1].

ACTIONS either are voluntary or involuntary. The difference between them is not of kind but of degree. Analyse the process of an involuntary action and you will find that if, for example, a man intends to thrust a needle in your eye or draws a sword to strike on your head, your eye in the former case will at once close and in the latter your hand will suddenly be raised up to shield your head. This prompt action on the part of your eye and hand is due to your consciousness of the evil to be evaded, and this gives rise to volition which moves the eye and the hand without the last delay. There are, however, cases the desirability or rejection of which needs meditation, but the moment mind decides, the decision is carried out as promptly as in the above example. This meditation translated into choice or rejection constitutes will. Now will makes its choice between two alternatives and takes its cue either from imagination or reason. For ex-

1. *Iḥya* IV. 5.

ample, a man be unable to cut his own throat, not because his hand is weak or a knife is not available, but because will is lacking which would give the stimulus to suicide. For man loves his own life. But suppose he gets tired of his life, owing to having harrowing pains and unbearable mental sufferings. He has now to choose between two alternatives which are both undesirable. A struggle commences and he hangs between life and death. If he thinks that death which will put an end to his sufferings quickly is preferable to life with its lingering intolerable pains, he will choose death although he loves his life. This choice gives rise to will, the command to which, communicated through proper channels, would then be faithfully executed by his hand in the manner of suicide. Thus, though the process from the commencement of mental struggle for the choice between two alternatives down to the stimulus to physical action is uniformly determinate there is, at any rate, a sort of freedom traceable in the will.

Man holds the balance between deteminism and freedom. The uniform succession of events is on the lines of determination but his choice which is an essential element of will is his own. Our Ulama have therefore coined a separate phrase : *Kasb* (acquisition), distinguishing it from *Jabr* (necessity) and *Ikhtiyar* (freedom). They say that fire burns of necessity (*Jabr*) but man may acquire fire through the appropriate methods, while in Almighty God is the ultimate cause of fire (*Ikhtiyar*). But it must be noted that when we use the word *Ikhtiyar* for God, we must exclude the notion of choice, which is an essential element of will in man. Let it be here recognised once for all as a general principle that all the words of man's vocabulary when used for God's attributes are similarly metaphorical.[2]

---

1. It is interesting to note here the following passage from a modern European author : If we form a conception of a Perfect or Infinite Mind it is in this sense that we must speak of such a mind as free. To speak of choice between alternatives is to suggest that another than the best might be chosen and this would be inconsistent with the idea of perfection.

A finite mind, limited in knowledge and power and distracted by desires other than the will to goodness, may yet have a partial measure of self-determination which is complete only in the infinite. It is incompletely determined by forces external to itself. And if it stand—as it does stand—between the realm of nature and the realm of goodness, conscious of the good and yet beset by many temptations to fall to a lower level, then the relative independence or partial spontaneity of such a mind may be exhibited in the power to direct its own path toward the goal of goodness or to allow it to lapse into evil. Its freedom will be neither complete independence of external determination nor complete agreement with the ideal of goodness ; but it will exclude total subordination to the forces beyond itself, and it will give opportunity for choosing and serving the good. In spite of

The question may be asked: If God is the ultimate cause, why should there be causal connection in the orderly succession of events? The answer to this lies in the correct understanding of the nature of causation. Nothing causes anything. Antecedents have consequents.[1] God alone is the efficient cause, but the ignorant have misunderstood and misapplied the word *power*. As to the orderly succession of events, let it be understood that the two events are conjoined like the relation between the condition and the conditioned. Now certain conditions are very apparent and can be known easily by people of little understanding, but there are conditions which are understood only by those who see through the light of intuition: hence the common error of miscalculating the uniformity of events. There is a divine purpose linking the antecedents to the consequents and manifesting itself in the existing orderly succession of events, without the least break or

---

its restrictions human activity will be recognized as possessing a core of spontaneity."—W. R. Sorley: *Moral Value and the Idea of God.* Cambridge 1918, pp. 446-7.

1. Ghazzali here anticipated Hume. "Seven hundred years before Hume, Ghazzali cut the bond of causality with the edge of his dialectic."—*Journal of the American Oriental Society.* Vol. XX 103.

irregularity. "Verily," says the Quran, "We did not create the heavens and the earth and what is between them in sport. We did not create them both but with truth, but most of them do not know."[1]

Surely, there is a set purpose pervading the universe. The uniform succession of events is not at random. There is no such thing as chance. Here again it may be asked: If God is the efficient cause, how will you account for actions attributed to man in the scriptures? Are we to believe that there are two causes for one effect? My answer to this will be that the word cause is vaguely understood. It can be used in two different senses. Just as we say that the death of A was caused by (1) B, the executioner, and (2) C, the king's order. Both these statements are correct. Similarly God is the cause of action as He has creative power and efficiency. At the same time man is the cause of actions as he is the source of the manifestation of uniform succession of events. In the former case we have a real causal connection, while in the latter a relation of the antecedent to the consequent after the manner of the connection between the

1. *Quran* XLIV. 38, 39.

condition and the conditioned. There are passages in the Quran where the word cause is used in different senses.

"The angel of death who is given charge of you shall cause you to die: then to your Lord you shall be brought back."[1] "Allah takes the souls at the time of their death."[2]

"Have you considered what you sow?"[3] "We pour down the water, pouring it down in abundance. Then We cleave the earth; cleaving it asunder. Then We cause to grow therein the grain."[4]

"Fight them: Allah will chastise them by your hands and bring them to disgrace."[5] "So you did not slay them, but it was Allah who slew them, and thou didst not smite when thou didst smite, but it was Allah who smote, that He might confer upon the Believers a good gift from Himself."[6]

---

1. *Quran* XXXII. 11.
3. *Quran* XXXIX. 42.
2. *Quran* LVI. 63.
4. *Quran* LXXX. 25-7.
5. *Quran* IX. 14.
6. *Quran* VIII. 17. This passage refers to the battle of Badr, the first battle of the Prophet. The Muslims slew the enemy but it is affirmed that really they did not slay, but it was Allah who slew them; the meaning apparently being that Allah's hand was working in the battle, which is also clear from the fact that three

These passages show that the word cause signifies creative power, and must be applied to God alone. But as man's power is the image of God's power the word was applied to him figuratively. Yet, just as the death of a culprit is caused by the actual killing by the hand of the executioner and not the king's order, so the word cause actually applied to man is contrary to fact. God alone is the real efficient cause, and the word must be applied to him in its root sense of power.

---

hundred Muslims, mostly raw and equipped with neither horses nor sufficient arms, prevailed against a thousand of the most renowned warriors who had come to crush the growing power of Islam. "And thou didst not smite when thou didst smite." Ghazzali points out that negation and affirmation for one and the same action throw new light on the nature of causation. Negation affirms God as the efficient and real cause; affirmation establishes man's free-will faithfully executing divine order.

"Whose branches are ever shaken by the wind,
And whose fruit is showered on the sleeper's heads.
Fatalism means sleeping amidst highwaymen.
Can a cock who crows too soon expect peace?
If ye cavil at and accept not God's hints,
Though ye count yourselves men, see, ye are women.
The quantum of reason ye possessed is lost,
And the head whose reason has fled is a till.
Inasmuch as the unthankful are despicable,
They are at last cast into the fiery pit.
If ye really have trust in God, exert yourselves,
And strive in constant reliance on the Almighty."

(Translation by E. Whinfield. *Masnavi*, 2nd ed. 1898 Bk. I. pp. 19-20.)

It may be asked then, why man should be rewarded for his good actions and punished for his misdeeds. Let us consider first the nature of reward and punishment. Experience tells us that things have natural properties and that physical laws operate in a uniform manner. Take, for example, the science of medicine. Certain drugs are found to possess certain qualities. If a man swallows poison of his own accord he has no right to ask why poison kills him. Its natural property has simply operated in his system and caused his death. Similarly actions make an impression on mind. Good and bad actions are invariably followed by pleasure and pain respectively. A good action is its own reward of pleasure and a bad one of pain. The former works like an elixir; the latter like poison. The properties of actions have been discovered, like discoveries in medicine, but by the physicians of the heart, the saints and the prophets. If you will not listen to them you must suffer the consequence. Now hear a parable:

A certain king sent a horse, a robe of honour, and travelling expenses to one of his suzerains in a distant land. Although the king had no need of his services, the royal gift was a favour shown to his suzerain, so that he might come to the king's court and be happy in his presence. If the suzerain understands the king's intention from the nature of the gift and utilizes it properly with a grateful heart, he will wait on the king and live happily, but if he misuses the gift or takes no heed of it, he will prove an ungrateful wretch.

It is thus that the boundless mercy of the omnipotent and omniscient God bestowed on us the gift of life, providing us with bodily organs, mental and moral faculties, so that we uplift ourselves by utilizing them properly, and be worthy of being admitted into His holy Presence. If we misuse them or pay no regard to them, surely we shall be Kafirs (literally "ungrateful") for His blessings bestowed on us for our good, and thus be doomed.

"Verily," says the Quran, "We created man in the best make. Then We render him the lowest of the low : Except those who believe and do good, so they shall have a reward never to be cut off."[1]

---

1. *Quran* XCV. 4-6. Whether man is by nature good or bad is a question which has vexed great thinkers from ancient times. Various answers have been suggested, which are summed up in three distinct theories :

The Allegory of the Pen

A certain devotee who was on the way to illumination saw a piece of paper with lines written on it. " Why," said the devotee, " hast thou blackened thy bright face ? " " It is not fair to take me to task " replied the paper. " I have

1. Evil is innate. Education simply muzzles the brute in man. Civilisation is mere veneering process. This cynical view of human natute is the religion of despair.

2. Man is neither good nor bad. Mind is a *tabula rasa.* Good or bad actions leave their impression. Thorns and roses are alike gathered by it.

3. Good and evil are mixed up in man. He has an angelic as well as a satanic nature. The development of this double nature depends on the force of external circumstances and surrounding influences. Good and evil are like two seeds : whichever is sown and taken care of will grow into a tree.

The Quranic expression : " We created man in the best make" emphasises the purity of his nature. He is born with good and for good, but has to preserve and to develop his goodness to his full capacity in the struggle of life. He has but one seed which is good ; if it grows and bears fruit it is called goodness ; if it be crushed or nipped in the bud it is called evil. Evil, therefore, has no separate entity in him, it is simply a negative which will lose his soul and reduce him to the lower depths.

It is interesting to note a parallel passage from the *Masnavi* of Jalaluddin Rumi, who was born in 1207 A.D. ninety-seven years after the death of Al Ghazzali.

" When a master places a spade in the hand of a slave,
The slave knows his meaning without being told.;
Like this spade, our hands are our Master's hints to us ;
Yea, if ye consider, they are His directions to us
When ye have taken to heart His hints,
Ye will shape your life in reliance on their direction ;
Wherefore these hints disclose His intent,

done nothing." "Ask the ink why she has sallied forth from the inkstand where she was quite at ease, and forcibly blackened my face." "You are right," said the devotee. Then he turned to the ink and enquired of her. "Why do you ask me?" she said. "I was sitting still in the inkstand and had no mind to come out but this truculent pen rushed at me, drew me out and scattered me over the page. There you see me lying helpless, go to the pen and ask him." The devotee turned to the pen and interrogated him about his high-handedness. "Why do you trouble me?" answered the pen. "Look, what am I? an insignificant reed. I was growing by the banks of silvery streams amidst shady green trees, when lo, a hand stretched at me. It held a knife, which uprooted me, flayed me and

---

Take the burden from you, and appoint your work,
He that hears it make it hearable by you,
He too is able to make it within your ability.
Accept His command and you will be able to execute it,
Seek union with Him and you will find yourselves united.
Exertion is giving thanks for God's blessings;
Think ye that your fatalism gives such thanks;
Giving thanks for blessings increases blessings
But fatalism snatches those blessings from your hands
Your fatalism is to sleep on the road; sleep not
Till ye behold the gates of the King's palace.
Ah! sleep not, unreflecting fatalists,
Till ye have reached that fruit-laden Tree of Life.

—E. Whinfield, trs. *Masnavi.*

separated my joints, hewed me, cleaved my head, then chopped it off. I was sent headlong towards the ink, and have to serve abjectly. Do not add insult to my injuries, go to the hand and ask him." The devotee looked at the hand and said: "Is it true? Are you so cruel?" "Do not be angry, sir," replied the hand. "I am a bundle of flesh, bones, and blood. Have you ever seen a piece of flesh exerting power? Can a body move of itself? I am a vehicle used by one called vitality. He rides on me and forces me round and round. You see, a dead man has hands but cannot use them because vitality has left them. Why should I, a mere vehicle, be blamed? Go to vitality and ask him why he makes use of me." "You are right," said the devotee, and then questioned vitality. "Do not find fault with me," answered vitality. "Many a time a censurer himself is reproved, while the censured is found faultless. How do you know that I have forced the hand? I was already there before he moved, and had no idea of the motion. I was unconscious and the onlookers were also unaware of me. Suddenly an agent came and stirred me. I had neither strength enough to disobey nor willingness to obey him. That for which you would take me to task I had to do according to his wish. I do not know who this agent is. He is called will and I know him by name only. Had the matter been left to me I think I should have done nothing." "All right," continued the devotee, "I shall put the question to will, and ask him why he has forcibly employed vitality which of its own accord would have done nothing." "Do not be in too great a hurry," exclaimed will. "Perchance I may give you sufficient reason. His majesty, the mind, sent an ambassador, named knowledge, who delivered his message to me through reason, saying: 'Rise up, stir vitality.' I was forced to do so, because I have to obey knowledge and reason, but I know not why. As long as I receive no order I am happy, but the moment an order is delivered I dare not disobey. Whether my monarch be a just ruler or a tyrant, I must obey him. On my oath, as long as the king hesitates or ponders over the matter I stand quiet, ready to serve, but the moment his order is passed my sense of obedience which is innate forces me to stir up vitality. So you should not blame me. Go to knowledge and get information there." 'You are right," consented the devotee, and proceeding, asked mind and its ambassadors, knowledge and reason, for an explanation. Reason excused himself by saying he was a lamp only, but knew not who had lighted it. Mind pleaded his innocence by calling himself a mere *tabula rasa*. Knowledge maintained that it was simply an inscription on the *tabula rasa*, inscribed after the lamp of reason had been lighted. Thus he could not be considered the author of the inscription which may have been the work of some invisible pen. The devotee was puzzled by the reply, but collecting himself, he spoke thus to knowledge: "I am wandering in the path of my enquiry. To whomsoever I go and ask the reason I am referred to another. Nevertheless, there is pleasure in my quest, for I find that everyone gives me a plausible reason. But pardon me, sir, if I say that your reply, knowledge, fails to satisfy me. You say that you are a mere inscription recorded by a pen. I have seen pen, ink, and tablet. They are of reed, a black mixture, and of wood and iron, respectively. And I have seen lamps lighted with fire. But here I do not see any of these things, and yet you talk of the tablet, the lamp, the pen and the inscription. Surely you are not trifling with me?" "Certainly not," returned knowledge. " I spoke in right earnest. But I see your difficulty. Your means are scanty, your horse is jaded, and your journey is long and dangerous. Give up this enterprise, as I fear you cannot succeed. If, however, you are prepared to run the risk, then listen. Your journey extends through three regions. The first is the terrestrial world. Its objects, pen, ink, paper, hand etc. are just what you have seen them to be. The second is the celestial world, which will begin when you have left me behind. There you will come across dense forests, deep wide rivers and high, impassable mountains and I know not how you would be able to proceed. Between these two worlds there is a third intermediary region called the phenomenal world. You have crossed three stages of it: vitality, will, and knowledge. To use a simile: a man who is walking is treading the terrestrial world : if he is sailing in a boat he enters the phenomenal world : if he leaves the boat and swims and walks on the waters, he is admitted in the celestial world. If you do not know how to swim, go back. For the watery region of the celestial world begins now when you can see that pen inscribing on the tablet of the heart. If you are not of whom it was said : 'O ye of little faith, wherefore didst thou doubt?'[1] prepare thyself. For by faith you shall not simply walk on the sea but fly in the air." The wondering devotee stood speechless for a while, then turning to knowledge, began: "I am in a difficulty. The dangers of the path which you have described unnerve my heart, and I know not whether I have sufficient strength to face them and to succeed in the end." "There is a test for your strength," replied knowledge. "Open your eyes and fix your gaze on me. If you see the pen which writes on the heart, you will, in my opinion, be able to proceed further on. For he who crosses the phenomenal world, knocks at the door of the celestial world, then sights the pen which writes on hearts." The devotee did as he was advised, but failed to see that pen, because his notion of pen was no other but of a pen of reed or wood. Then knowledge drew his atten-

---

1. *St. Matthew* XIV 55-31. "And in the fourth watch of the night he came unto them, walking on the sea. And when the disciples saw him walking on the sea, they were troubled saying, It is an apparition and they cried out for fear. But straightway Jesus spoke unto them, saying: Be of good cheer, it is I, be not afraid. And Peter answered him and said: Lord, if it be thou, bid me come unto thee upon the water. And Peter went down from the boat and walked upon the waters to come to Jesus. But when he saw the wind he was afraid, and beginning to sink he cried saying, Lord, save me. And immediately Jesus stretched forth his hand, and took hold of him and said unto him: O thou of little faith, wherefore didst thou doubt?"

tion, saying: "There's the rub. Do you not know that the furniture of a palace indicates the status of its lord? Nothing in the universe resembles God, therefore His attributes are also transcendental. He is neither body nor is in space. His hand is not a bundle of flesh, bone, and blood. His pen is not of reed or wood. His writing is not from ink prepared from vitriol and gall. But there are many who ignorantly cling to an anthropomorphic view of Him, there are few who cherish a transcendentally pure conception of Him, and believe that He is not only above all material limitation but even above the limitation of metaphor. You seem to be oscillating between these two views, because on the one hand you think that God is immaterial, that His words have neither sound nor shape; on the other hand you cannot rise to the transcendental conception of His hand, pen and tablet. Do you think that the meaning of the tradition "Verily God created Adam in His own image" is limited to the visible face of man? Certainly not: it is the inward nature of man seen by the inward sight which can be called the image of God. But, listen: You are

1. Comp. *Quran* XLII. 11: Nothing is like a likeness of Him. He is the Hearing, the Seeing.

2. Comp. *Genesis* I. 27.

now at the sacred mount, where the invisible voice from the burning bush speaks: 'I am that I am;[1] " Verily I am thy Lord God, put off thy shoes."[2] The devotee, who listening with rapture, suddenly saw as it were a flash of lightning, there appeared working the pen which writes on hearts, formless. "A thousand blessings on thee, O knowledge, who hast saved me from falling into the abysm of anthropomorphism (*Tashbih*). " I thank thee from the bottom of my heart. I tarried long, but now, adieu! "

The devotee then resumed his journey. Halting in the presence of the invisible pen, politely he asked the same question: "You know my reply," answered the mysterious pen. "You cannot have forgotten the reply given to you by the pen in the terrestrial world." " Yes, I remember," replied the devotee, "but how can it be the same reply, because there is no similitude between you and that pen." "Then it seems you have for-

1. *Exodus* III. 14.

2. *Quran* XX. 12. It is generally supposed that Moses was ordered to take off his " leather shoes " out of respect for the sacred place. But Razi in his Commentary calls it an idiom and says that the Arabs used the word Na'al (shoe) for wife and family. The command to put off the shoes is therefore a metaphorical expression for making the heart vacant from care of family: See *Tafsir-i-Razi*, vol. VI, 19. Stamboul edition.

gotten the tradition: Verily God created Adam in His own image." "No, sir," interrupted the devotee. "I know it by heart." "And you have frogotten also that passage in the Quran : " And the heavens rolled up in His right hand."[1] " Certainly not," exclaimed the devtee, " I can repeat the whole of the Quarn by the rote." "Yes, I know, and as you are now treading the sacred precincts of the celestial world I think I can now safely tell that you have simply learnt the meaning of these passages from a negative point of view. But they have a positive value, and should be utilised as constructive at this stage[2] Proceed further and you will understand what I mean." The devotee looked and found himself reflecting upon the divine attribute omnipotence. At once he realised the force of the mysterious pen's argu-

---

1. *Quran* XXXIX. 97. The full text runs: And they have not honoured Allah with the honour due to Him : and the whole earth shall be in His grip on the day of resurrection and the heavens rolled up in His right hand ; glory be to Him and may He be exalted above what they associate with Him.

2. Ghazzali has dealt with the question fully in his work entitled 'Iljamal awam.' He says that every object has four stages of existence. To use a figure : " Fire " is (1) written on paper : (2) pronounced as Fire (3) burns ; and (4) is perceived by the mind to be inflammable. The first two are purely conventional but have an educational value. Similarly the anthropomorphism of the passages of the Scriptures should be studied in the light of the above stages.

ment, but goaded by his inquisitive nature he was about to put the question to the holy being, when a voice like the deafening sound of thunder was heard from above, proclaiming : " He is not questioned for his actions but they shall be asked." Filled with surprise, the devotee bent his head in silent submission.

The hand of the divine mercy stretched towards the helpless devotee ; into his ear were whispered in zephyr tones : "Verily those who strive in Our way We will certainly show them the path which leads to Us."[1] Opening his eyes, the devotee raised his head and poured forth his heart in silent prayer : " Holy art Thou, O God Almighty : blessed is Thy name, O Lord of the universe ! Henceforth I shall fear no mortal : I put my entire trust in Thee : Thy forgiveness is my solace : Thy mercy is my refuge. "

(Light may be thrown on the matter by consideration of the unity of God.)[2]

---

1. *Quran* XXIX. 69.
2. See Section VI. of this book.

PRIDE AND VANITY*

WHEN a man feels a superiority over others and with this sort of inward elation, this is called pride. It differs from vanity inasmuch as vanity means consciousness of one's elation while pride requires a subject, an object and a feeling of elation. Suppose a man is born solitary in the world, he may be vain but not proud, because in pride man considers himself superior to others for certain qualities of his self. He allots one position to his self and one to another, and then thinks that his position is higher and is therefore elated. This " puffed up " feeling which imparts a sense of " touch me not " is called pride. The Prophet says: 'O God, save me from the puffing up of pride." Ibn Abbas says that the sentence in the Quran, " And they have pride in their hearts and will fail to reach it " means that the thought of inward greatness will be denied to them. This thought is the source of inward and outward actions, which are so to speak the fruits of it.

* *Ihya* III. 9.

A proud man will not tolerate any other to be on equal terms with himself. In private and in public he expects that all should assume a respectful attitude towards him and acknowledging his superiority treat him as a higher being. They should greet him first, make way for him wherever he walks; when he speaks everyone should listen to him and never try to oppose him. He is a genius and people are like asses. They should be grateful to him seeing that he is so condescending. Such proud men are found especially among the Ulama. Sages are ruined by their pride. The Prophet says: " He who has an atom of pride in his heart will fail to enter paradise." This saying requires explanation, and should be carefully listened to. Virtues are the doors of Paradise, but pride and self-esteem lock them all. So long as man feels elated he will not like for others what he likes for himself. His self-esteem will deprive him of humility, which is the essence of righteousness. He will neither be able to discard enmity and envy, resentment and wrath, slander and scorn, nor will he be able to cultivate truth and sincerity, and calmly listen to any advice. In short, there is no evil which a proud man will not inevitably do in order to preserve his elation and self-esteem. Vices are like a chain of rings linked together which entangle his heart. Therefore, an atom of pride is Satan's spark, which secretly consumes the nature of the sons of Adam.

Know then that pride is of three kinds: 1. Against God; 2. Against prophets and saints; 3. Against fellow men.

1. Against God. It is due to mere foolishness when a biped creature considers himself as if Lord of the universe. Namrud and Pharaoh were such types, who disdained to be called God's creatures on earth: "Verily, verily," says the Quran," the Messiah does by no means disdain that he should be a servant of Allah, nor do the angels who are near to Him, and whoever disdains His service and is proud He will gather them all together to Himself."[1]

2. Against prophets and saints. It is due to unwarranted self-esteem when one considers obedience to any mortal being as lowering his own position. Such a person either fails to reflect on the nature of prophetship and thereby feels proud of himself and does not obey a

---

1. *Quran* IV. 172.

prophet, or refuses to consider the claims of prophetship as being derogatory to his elated self and therefore pays no regard to a prophet. The Quran quotes the words of such persons :— "And they say: what is the matter with this Apostle that he eats food and goes about in the markets, why has not an angel been sent down to him so that he should have been a warner with him? Or (why is not) a treasure sent down to him or he is made to have a garden from which he should eat." "And those who do not fear our meeting, say: why have not angels been sent down to us, or (why) do we not see our Lord? Now certainly they are too proud of themselves and have revolted in great revolt."[1]

Our Prophet Muhammad was an orphan and had scanty means of livelihood, so the Koraishite chief Walid bin Moghera and Abu Masood Sakfi used to speak contemptuously of him.[2] And when people believed in him and accepted Islam, the proud Koraishites used to say: Muhammad is surrounded by poor men, let him

1. *Quran* XXV. 7, 8 ; 21.

2. *Quran* XLIII. 31. And they say : why was not this Quran revealed to a man of importance in the two towns." (Mecca and Taif).

send them off and then we of the aristocracy of Mecca will listen to him. But God spoke to Muhammad, "And withhold thyself with those who call on their Lord morning and evening, desiring His good will, and let not their eyes pass from them, desiring the beauties of this world's life, and do not follow him, whose heart We have made unmindful to Our resemblance, and he follows his low desires, and his case is one in which due bounds are exceeded."[1]

3. Against fellow men. A proud man considers himself a superior being and would like to see everybody humbled before him. He is therefore quarelling with God, trying to share with Him His attribute omnipotence. God is spoken of in the Hadith as saying : Omnipotence is my mantle, he who quarrels with me for it, him will I crush." Surely men are all His servants and no servant has a right to treat his fellow servants as their master. But a proud man in the intoxication of his elation takes himself as God on earth. He is too haughty to listen to truth from the lips of any of his fellow men. Ibn Masood says : "It is enough for sin if a

1. *Quran* XVIII. 28.

person, who is advised to fear God answers his adviser : Look to thine own self."

The consciousness of superiority which begets pride is due to certain attributes or accomplishments which can be summed up as :

(*a*) Spiritual, divided into (1) knowledge ; (2) devotion.

(*b*) Worldly, of five kinds : (3) pedigree ; (4) beauty ; (5) strength ; (6) wealth ; (7) kith and kin.

There are thus seven causes in all, and these need some description.

Knowledge is power. Consciousness of power easily elates a man, who considers himself superior to others and treats them in a supercilious manner. If he accepts the greetings or the invitation of his fellow men or receives them in audience he thinks they should be thankful to him for his condescension. People should obey and serve him, for by virtue of his knowledge he thinks he has a right over them. Such a proud "Alim" is sorry for the sins of others but unmindful of his own condition. While he freely distributes Heaven and Hell among his fellow men, he claims salvation and Heaven for himself. The question is whether he is really justified in holding the title of *Alim*. For an

Alim is one who, knowing himself knows God, who fears the Lord most, who holds himself more responsible for his actions for he knows good and evil and feels the awful presence of a mighty and just Being who looks to righteousness alone.

Let us consider why men of knowledge become proud. There are two main causes which should be noted. First there is a false conception about the nature of real knowledge. Devoted to certain sciences and arts such as mathematics, physics, literature, and dialectics, they think that proficiency in them makes a man perfect. But real knowledge means the lifting of the veil from before the eyes of the heart so as to see the mysterious relation between man and his Maker and to be filled with a sense of awe and reverence in the presence of an omniscient holy Being who pervades the universe. This attitude of mind, this enlightenment, is real knowledge. It produces humility and repels pride.

Secondly, there is an indifference to moral training during student life. Wicked habits thus produce bitter fruits of pride. Wahb has well illustrated this point, when he says: "Knowledge is like rain falling from above, so pure and sweet but the plants when they absorb it, embitter or sweeten it, according to their tastes. Man in acquiring knowledge acquires power, which gives strength to the hidden qualities of his heart. If he was prone towards pride and paid no attention to the subjugation of it, he would prove more proud when he acquires knowledge." "There will be men," says the Prophet, "who will have the Quran on their lips but it will not go down their throats. They will claim knowledge of it, calling themselves learned Qari. They will be from among you, my companions, but woe to them, for thee will see the consequence of it in Hell."[1]

Warned by their Prophet, his companions lived a life of humility and their example taught its lesson to their successors. A person came to Khalif Omar after morning prayers and said: "I should like to give public sermons." "My friend," said the Khalif, "I am afraid you would soon be puffed up with pride." Huzaifa, the compannion of the Prophet, was a leader of prayer. One day he said to his congregation: "Brethren, have another leader, or go and pray alone, for I begin to feel puffed up with your leadership."

1. Ibn Ibbas.

Thus, the companions of the Prophet lived meekly, the humble servants of God on earth, keenly watching the changing phases of their hearts and promptly seeking the remedy. But we who call ourselves their followers not only do not try to purify our hearts but do not even think it worth while to consider the means for their purification. How can we expect salvation? But we ought not to lose heart. The Apostle of Mercy for the worlds (Rahmat ul lilalamin) has said: "Soon a time will come when if any person will do even one-tenth of what you are doing now, he will have his salvation."[1]

Devotion and religious service elicit admiration and praise for the devotee, who finding himself respected by the people is elated. This elation quietly develops into pride and then the devotee considers himself a superior being and favoured of God. He despises his fellow men and calls them sinners, who will be doomed for ever. But he does know that he himself will be doomed for despising his fellow men and thinking too much of himself. The Prophet says: "When you hear any person, saying: 'woe to

1. Tirmizi: Abu Huraira's report.

the people they are doomed,' know that he himself will be doomed first."

It is recorded that a certain sinner among the Jews passed by a well known Pharisee. Struck with the appearance of the Pharisee's piety and devotion, the poor sinner sat down by him, believing in the saving grace of his holy touch. But the proud Pharisee disdainfully spoke out : "Touch me not, thou filthy sinner, and leave my presence." Whereupon God sent His word to the prophet of that age : " Go and tell that sinner thou art forgiven. As for that Pharisee, his devotion is cast aside and he is doomed."

3. People are usually proud of their lineage, and look down on men of low birth. They refuse to treat them on equal terms, and boastfully speak of their ancestors in the presence of men, who are treated by them in a haughty manner. This evil lurks even in the hearts of good and virtuous men, although their manners and actions throw a veil over it. But in an unguarded moment of excitement and fury, this demon of pedigree is let loose from the innermost corner of the heart.

The Prophet's companion Abuzar says : "I was quarrelling with someone in the presence of the Prophet when suddenly in a fit of rage I abused the man saying, Thou son of a negress!" On this the Prophet coaxingly said to me: "Abuzar, both the scales are equal. The white has no preference over the black." Hearing this I fell and said to the person: Brother, come and trample on my face and then forgive me.

It is reported in the Hadith that two men were quarrelling before the Prophet. One said to the other: "I am the son of such and such illustrious man, tell me who thy father is." The Prophet, addressing the boastful man said: "There were two men in the time of Moses who boastfully spoke of their pedigree. One said to the other: Look, how my nine ancestors all in one line were men of renown. And God said to Moses: "Tell this man all thy nine ancestors are in Hell and thou art the tenth."

4. Women generally feel proud of their beauty. This leads to finding fault with others, and this gradually assumes the form of contempt and disdain. Ayesha, the wife of the Prophet, says: "One day a woman came to the Prophet and I said to him: "Look at this dwarf!" The Prophet turned towards me and said: 'Ayesha, repent of what thou hast said, for it is slander.'

5, 6, 7. People feel a sort of elation at the sight of their possessions. A merchant is elated with his stores, a landowner with his fields and groves, and a nobleman with his retinue and riches. In short, every person feels proud of his worldly possessions and looks down on those who are lacking in them. He believes in riches and worships mammon.[1] He has no idea of what is meant by: "Blessed are the poor in spirit: for theirs is the kingdom of Heaven."[2]

We may quote a parable from the Quran: "And set forth to them a parable of two men. For one of them We made two gardens of grape-vines, and We surrounded them both with palms, and in the midst of them We made corn-fields. Both these gardens yielded their fruits and failed nothing. We caused a river to gush forth in their midst. The man possessed much wealth and he said to his companion while he disputed with him: I have greater wealth than you and am mightier in followers. While he entered his garden he was unjust to himself. He said: I do

1. Comp. *Matt.* VI. 24: "No man can serve two masters for either he will hate the one and love the other; or else he will hold to the one and despise the other. Ye cannot serve God and mammon."

2. *Matt.* V. 3.

not think that this will ever perish. I do not think the hour will come, yet even if I return to my Lord I shall most certainly find a place better than this. His companion said to him, while disputing with him : Do you disbelieve in Him who created you from dust, then from a small germ life, then he made you a perfect man ? But as for me, Allah is my Lord and I do not associate any one with my Lord. When you entered your garden, why did you not say : It is as Allah has pleased. There is no power save Allah If you consider me to be inferior to you in wealth and children, perhaps my Lord will give me something better than your garden, and send on it a reckoning from heaven, so that it shall become even ground with no living plant. Or the waters may sink into the ground so that you are unable to find them. His wealth was indeed destroyed, and he bagan to wring his hands for what he had spent on it. While it lay there (for it had fallen down from the roofs) he said : Ah me ! would that I had not associated anyone with my Lord. He had none to help him besides Allah nor could he defend himself. In Allah, alone is protection, the True One. In the bestowal of reward and in requital He is best.

Set forth to them also the parable of the life in this world. It is like the water which We send down from the clouds on account of which the herbs become luxuriant. Then these become dry, break into pieces and the winds scatter them. Allah holds power over all things. Wealth and children are an adornment of the life of this world. The good works, the ever-abiding, are with your Lord better in reward than in expectation."[1]

How fleeting are our worldly gains, and how foolish are we in feeling proud of them ! Let us then live as meek and humble servants of God on earth.

---

1. *Quran* XVIII. 32-46.

FRIENDSHIP AND SINCERITY*

FRIENDSHIP is one of God's favours. Says the Quran, " And hold fast by the covenant of Allah all together and be not disunited, and remember the favour of Allah on you when you were enemies, then He united your hearts so by His favour you became brethren.[1] The Prophet says: Those amongst you are my close companions, who have good dispositions, are affectionate and tenderly love each other. And again: " God when He shows His kindness towards any person gives him a good friend."[2] " Verily God will say on the day of Resurrection, where are those who loved each other for My sake; to-day they shall rest under My shelter when there is no other shelter."[3]

" Seven kinds of men will, on the Day of Judgment, rest under His shelter when there will be no other shelter:—(1) A just Imam. (2) An adult who is devoted to God. (3) A man

---

*Ihya 115; IV. 7.

1. Quran III. 102.
2. Tibrami and Abu Daud.
3. Muslim.

who after coming out from the mosque finds his heart attached to it till he enters again. (4) Two friends who lived and died in their friendship for God's sake. (5) He who for fear of the Lord wept in secret. (6) He whom a beautiful woman of good birth allures but he replies: I have fear of my Lord. (7) He who gives alms in a manner that his left hand does not know what is given by his right hand."

Friendship, then, is God's favour and should be cultivated for His sake. But if we shun the company of our fellow men let it also be for God's sake. "The strongest rope of Faith," says the Prophet, "is love and hate both for God's sake."

Christ says, "Love God by avoiding the wicked; seek His nearness by shunning their company and please Him by courting their displeasure." With whom should we keep company, O Word of God," asked the people. And Christ replied, "Sit with those whose appearances remind you of God, whose words add to the stock of your knowledge and whose actions serve as an incentive for acquiring the Kingdom of Heaven."

God spoke to Moses saying, "Son of Amran! be up and find out a friend for thee and he who would not be with thee for my good will is thy enemy."

Choose a friend who has five qualities *viz.*, wisdom ; good disposition : abstinence from sin, heresy and greed.

A fool's company gives no good, it ends in gloom. Good disposition is necessary inasmuch as a man may be wise but be subservient to his inordinate passions and hence unfit for company. And a sinner and a heretic are to be avoided for the simple reason that they who have no fear of the Lord and are regardless of committing forbidden actions are not to be relied on. Besides, contagion will secretly spread and he too will think of sin lightly and gradually lose power of resisting it. And a greedy worldling is to be avoided because his company will deaden the heart in the quest of the Kingdom of Heaven.

Alkama on his death-bed gave a fine description of a friend. " My son," said he, " if you wish to keep company try to find out such a friend who, when you live with him, defends you, adds to your prestige, bears the load of your hardships, helps you in your doings, counts your virtues, dissuades you from vices, readily responds to your requests, inquires himself for your needs when you keep quiet; shows his deep sympathy in your sufferings; bears witness to your sayings; gives good advice when you intend to do some work and prefers you to his own self when difference arises between you and him." This piece of advice gives the qualities of a friend in a nutshell. When Caliph Mamun the Abbasid heard of it, he said: "Where should we find such a friend?" And Yahya replied, "Alkama's description means that we should live in retirement."

Imam Jafar 'Alsadiq' (the veracious) gives a negative description of a friend. "Do not keep company with five sorts of men *viz.*, a false man who deceives you like a mirage; a fool who cannot benefit you, (even if he tries to do so he would do harm through his foolishness); a miser who when you need his help the most, severs himself from you; a coward who will leave you when you are in danger; a wicked sinner who will sell you for a piece of bread."

Sahl of Taster says, "Avoid the company of three kinds of men, (1) tyrants who forget God, (2) Ulama who practise dissimulation, (3) Sufis who are ignorant."

It must be remembered here that the

above passages serve as an ideal but for purposes we should look to the present practical conditions and try to get as much good as may be had from them. For man's life seems dreary when he has no friends. And men are like trees. Some are fruit-bearing and shady, some are shady only and some are mere thorns and thistles. Similarly some friends are a blessing both here and hereafter ; some are for worldly gain for the world is a shadow, and some are of no good in this world and the next as if they are scorpions in human form.

"And they were not enjoined anything except that they should serve Allah, being sincere to Him in obedience, upright, and keep up prayer and pay the poor rate (Zakat) and that is the right religion."[1] "Then serve God, being sincere in religion unto Him. Aye, God's is the sincere religion." Musab says that his father Saad was considering himself superior to other poor and destitute companions of the Prophet. "God," said the Prophet, "has helped my people with my poor and humble followers' prayer and sincerity."[2] "Sincere action," says the Prophet, "even if it be little will suffice

1. *Quran* XVIII. 5.
2. Nasai and Bukhari.

for thee."[1] The following saying of the Prophet is reported by Abu Huraira: "Three persons shall be questioned first on the day of Resurrection. One will be the learned man who would be asked as to what he had done with his learning." "Day and night," the learned man will reply, "I tried my best to propagate it, O Lord." "Thou speakest falsely," God will answer and the angels will also join with Him. "Thy sole aim was to be called a learned man by the people, and the title was thine." The second will be the rich man who would be asked about his riches. "Day and night," the rich man will reply, "I gave it in charity." "Thou speaker of untruth," God and His angels will say, "thou wishest to be labelled a generous man, and it was done." The third will be the martyr who too will be asked about his deed. "O Lord," the martyr will reply, "Thou didst command us to wage holy war (Jehad). I obeyed Thee and fell fighting." "Thou liest," God and His angels will answer. "Thy aim was to be trumpeted as a hero and it was done." "Then," says Abu Huraira, "the Prophet after finishing the sermon pressed me and said: These three

---

1. Abu Mansur.

would be the first to be thrown into the flames of Hell."

In the narratives of the Israelites, a story is told of a certain devotee who had served God for many years. Once he was informed of the apostasy of a tribe, which, forsaking the true worship of Yahweh, had taken to tree worship. The hermit filled with the spirit of the "jealous" God took an axe and set out to level the tree to the earth. But the devil in the shape of an old man met him on the way and inquired of his intention. The hermit told him of his determination, whereupon Satan addressed him thus: "Why on earth are you leaving aside your prayers and vigils and devoting yourself to other work?" "But this too is a sacred cause," replied hermit. "No, nor will I allow you to do so," exclaimed the devil. Whereupon the hermit in the white heat of his pious rage caught hold of the devil and forcibly held him down. "Spare me, sir," begged the devil, "I have something to say to you." The hermit let him go. Then spoke Satan: "I think God has not commanded you to do this thing. You do not worship the tree, you are not responsible for the sins of others. If God wills it He will send some prophet, and they are so many, who would carry out his order. So I think it is not your duty, why then trouble yourself?" "But I belong to the chosen people of Yahweh, and I am in duty bound to do so," replied the hermit. Whereupon they again began to wrestle and eventually Satan was thrown down. "Oh! I see," cried Satan. "An idea has just come into my mind; let me go, please, and I will telly ou." Thus obtaining his release, the Evil One addressed him as follows: "Is it not the case that you are poor and have to live on the alms of those who are devoted to you? But in your heart of hearts you would like to shower your bounties on your brethren and neighbours, so generous and compassionate is your nature. What a pity that such a noble soul lives on alms." "You have read my mind aright," quietly responded the hermit. "May I hope," said the Evil One entreatingly, "that you will be pleased to accept two golden dinars which you will find at your side bed every morning from tomorrow. You will then be relieved of depending on others and be in a position to do charity to your poor relations and brethren. As for that wretched tree, what if that be cut down? Surely your poor, needy brethren would get nothing and you would lose the opportunity of helping them while the tree would grow again." The hermit prondered over these words and said to himself, "This old man speaks quite reasonably, but let me think over the pros and cons of the case. Am I a prophet? No, I am not; therefore I am not bound to cut it down. Am I commanded to do so? No Then if I do not do it I shall not be guilty of the iniquity. Should I accept his proposal? No doubt from the religious point of view it is more useful. No doubt. I think I should accept it: yes, I must." Thus the two pledged their words and the hermit returned. Next morning he found the two dinars at his bed side and was highly pleased. Another morning the glittering gold was there, but on the third morning the hermit searched for them in vain. His fury knew no bounds. He rushed for his axe, and hurried with it towards the place of idolatry. Satan again met him in the way as before. "Thou wretch, thou archdevil," cried out the hermit, "wilt thou prevent me from my sacred duty?" "You cannot do it, you dare not do it," retorted the Evil One. "Hast thou forgotten the test of my powers?" sharply replied the infuriated hermit and rushed at him. But to his great discomfort and humiliation the hermit instantly fell flat on the ground like a dry leaf from a tree. The devil planted his foot on his chest, holding him by the throat, dictating the following terms : " Either swear not to touch that tree or be prepared to die." The hermit finding himself quite helpless said, " I swear, but tell me why I am so discomfitured." " Listen," answered Satan. " At first thy wrath was for God's sake, and zealous vindication of His commandments, hence I was defeated. But now thou art furious for thyself, and worldly gain." The story illustrates the saying, " I will certainly cause them all to deviate from the way except thy servants from among those who are sincere." A devotee cannot be immune from Satan's temptation except by sincerity and therefore saint Maaruf of Karkh used to upbraid himself, saying : " If thou wishest salvation, be sincere."

Yacub the Sufi, says : "He who conceals his virtues like vices, is sincere." In a dream a man saw a Sufi who was dead and inquired about the actions of his previous life. "All those actions," said the Sufi, "which were for God's sake I was rewarded for, even the least of them. For example, I had thrown aside a pomegranate's peel from the thoroughfare. I lost my ass worth one hundred dinars, and a silken thread on my cap was found on the side of iniquities. Once I gave something in charity, and was pleased to see people looking at me,—this action has neither reward nor punishment for me." "How is it that you lost your ass ?" said the man to the Sufi. "Because," responded the latter, " when I heard of the death of my ass I said : 'damn it.' I ought to have thought of God's will." Saint Sufyan Saori, when he heard of this dream, said, "The Sufi was fortunate as no punishment was meted out to him for that charity which pleased him when people watched him."

There is a report that a man, putting on a woman's dress, used to frequent purdah parties in marriage and funeral processions. Once a lady's pearl was lost in a party. Everybody was being closely searched, and the man was very much afraid of the disclosure of his identity, as it would mean the loss of his life. He sincerely repented in his heart, never to do the same thing again, and asked God's forgiveness and help. Then he found that it was now the turn of himself and his companion to be searched. His prayer was heard, the pearl being found in his companion's clothes and he was saved.[1]

A Sufi narrates the following story: " I joined a naval squadron which was going on holy war (Jehad). One of us was selling his provision bag, and I bought it, thinking it would prove useful in the war, and that when the war was over I might dispose of it with profit. That same night I dreamt that two angels came down from heaven. One of them said to the other: Make a complete list of the crusaders. The other began to write down: So and so goes so a trip; so and so for trading, so and so for reputation; so and so for God's sake. Then he looked at me saying: Put this man down as trader. But I spoke: For God's sake do not misrepresent me. I am not going for business. I have no capital. I have simply started for the holy war. "But, sir," said the angel, " did you not buy that provision bag yesterday, and were you not thinking of making some profit?" I wept and entreated them not to put me down as a trader. The angel looked at the other, who said: "Well, write thus: This man set out for the holy war, but on the way bought a pro-

1. Rumi has beautifully described this story of Nasuh in *Masnavi* Bk. V.

vision bag for profiting : now God will judge the man."

Saint Sirri as-Saqati : "Two rakaats of prayer offered with sincerity in seclusion are better than copying seventy or seven hundred traditions with the complete list of authorities. Some say that one moment's sincerity is salvation, but it is very rare. Knowledge is the seed, practice is the crop, and sincerity is the water nourishing it. Some say that God's displeasure is revealed in a person who is given three things ; and is denied the same number. He gets access into the society of the virtuous, but derives no benefit therefrom. He performs good actions but lacks sincerity. He learns philosophy but fails to understand truth. Says a Sufi : " God looks to sincerity only, and not to the action of His creatures." Says Junaid : " There are some servants of God who are wise, who act as wise men, who are sincere when they act, then sincerity leads them to virtue."

Says Sahl : " Sincerity means that all our actions or intentions—all the states of our minds whether we are doing anything or at rest, be solely for God." But this is very difficult to acquire as it does not in the least attract the ego itself. Ruyam says: "Sincerity means disregard of recompense for action in both the worlds." In this he wishes to point out that the gratifications of our sensuous desires whether in this world or the next are all insignificant and low. He who worships God in order to attain joy in Paradise is not sincere. Let him act for God's "Riza." This stage is reached by *Siddiks* (sincerely devoted to God), and is sincerity *par excellence*. He who does good actions for fear of hell or hope of heaven is sincere inasmuch as he gives up at present his sensual worldly enjoyments, but wishes for the future the gratification of his appetite and passion in Paradise. The longing of true devotees is their Beloved's Riza. It may be objected here that men's motive is pleasure, that freedom from such pleasures is a purely divine attribute. But this objection is based on misunderstanding. It is true that man desires pleasure but pleasure has different meanings. The popular view is gratification of sensuous desires in Paradise but it has no idea of the nature of higher pleasures of communion and beatitude or the vision of God, and hence fails to consider them as pleasures. But these are the pleasures and he who enjoys them will not even look to the popular pleasures of Paradise for his highest pleasure, his *summum bonum*, is the love of God.

Tufail says : " To do good for men's sake is hypocrisy ; not to do is infidelity ; sincere is he who is free from both and works for God only." These definitions suggest the ideal of sincerity aimed at by noble souls. Let us now look to the practical side of it for the sake of the average man.

Actions make an impression on the heart, and strengthen that quality of it which served as a stimulus for them. For example, hypocrisy deadens the heart and Godly motive leads to salvation. Both of them will gather strength in proportion to the actions which proceed from their respective sources. But as they are intrinsically opposed to each other an action which gets an equal stimulus at one and the same time will be stationary in its effect on the heart. Now take a mixed action which draws the doer nearer to virtue, say, by one span, but removes him away by two spans, the inward result of his progress will be that he would remain where he was, although he would be rewarded or punished according to his motive. A man starts for " Haj " but takes with him some articles for trade ; he will get his reward of pilgrimage but if his motive was trade only, he could not be considered a "Haji." A crusader who fights for his religion would have his recompense although he acquires booty, for so long as his sole motive is to uphold the cause of religion, the latent desire of booty would not come in the way of his recompense. Granted that he is inferior to those noble souls who are wholly absorbed in Him—"who see through Him, who hear through Him who act through Him" (Hadis)—He still belongs to the good and the virtuous. For if we apply the highest standard to all, religion will be considered a hopeless task, and will ultimately be reduced to pessimism.

At the same time we must sound a note of warning for those who are satisfied with the low standard. They are very often deceived. They consider their motive is purely for God's sake while in reality they aim at some hidden sensuous pleasure. Let a doer, after he has exerted himself and pondered over his motive, be not overconfident of his sincerity. With the fear of its rejection let him hope for its acceptance—this is the creed of the righteous who fears the Lord and hopes from Him.

THE NATURE OF LOVE*

EXPERIENCES are either agreeable and therefore desired or disagreeable and avoided. Inclination towards a desired object when deeply rooted and strong constitutes love. Knowledge and perception of the beloved is the first requisite for love which is consequently divided according to the division of the five senses each of which is inclined towards its desired object. Thus the eye apprehends beautiful forms, the ear harmonious sounds, etc. This kind of experience we share with the animals. There is, however, one more sense, peculiar to man, which delights the soul. The Prophet has said: "I desire three things from your world: sweet smell, tender sex, and prayer, which is the delight of my eye." Now prayer is neither smelt nor touched, in fact, its delight is beyond the scope of the five senses and yet it has been described as the "delight of my eye," which means the inner eye—the soul with her sixth sense. Concepts of this special sense are more

---

*Ihya IV. 6.

beautiful and charming than sensuous objects, nay, they are more perfect and strongly attract the soul. Is it not, then, possible, that one who is not perceived by the five senses may yet be found and felt attractive by that sense and loved by the soul?

Let us now enumerate the circumstances which excite love. 1. Every living being first of all loves his own self, that is to say, the desire for continuity of his existence as opposed to annihilation is innate. This desire is augmented by the desire of the perfection of his self by means of sound body, wealth, children, relations and friends. For all of these serve as a means to the end of the continuity of his self and therefore he cherishes love for them. Even "unselfish" love of his dear son, if probed, smacks of love for the continuity of his self, because his son who is part of his self serves as a living representative of his self's continuity.

2. The second cause is the love for one's benefactor towards whom the heart is naturally attracted. Even if he be a stranger, a benefactor will always be loved. But it must be remembered that the benefactor is loved not for himself but for his beneficence, the extent of which will

be a dominating factor in determining the degree of love.

3. The third cause is love of beauty. It is generally supposed that beauty consists in red and white complexions, well proportioned limbs, and so forth, but we can also say "beautiful writing," "beautiful horse," etc. Hence beauty of an object consists in its possession of all possible befitting perfections. It will vary in proportion to the perfections attained. That writing in which all the rules of calligraphy are properly observed will be called beautiful and so on. At the same time there can be no one standard for judging the beauty of different objects. The standard for a horse cannot be the same for, say, writing or man. It must also be remembered that beauty is not connected with sensible objects only but is also related to concepts. A person is not always loved for his external beauty, but often the beauty of his knowledge or virtues attract the heart. It is not necessary that the object of such kind of love be perceived by the senses. We love our saints, imams, and prophets but we have never seen them. Our love for them is so strong that we would willingly lay down our lives for upholding

their good name. If we wish to create love for them in young minds we can produce it by giving graphic accounts of their virtues. Stories of the heroes of any nation will excite love for them.

"Love looks not with the eyes but with the mind; and therefore is winged Cupid, painted blind."

4. The fourth cause is a sort of secret affinity between two souls, meeting and attracting each other. It is what is called "love at first sight." This is what the Prophet meant when he said, "The souls had their rendezvous: Those who liked each other then, love here; those who remained strangers then, do not join here."[1] If a believer goes to a meeting where there are a hundred munafiks (hypocrites) and one momin (faithful) he will take his seat by the side of the momin. It seems that likes are attracted by their likes. Malik bin Dinar says: Just as birds of the same feather fly together two persons having a quality common to both will join.

Let us now apply these causes and find out who may be the true object of love. First, man who is directly conscious of his own self in whom the love for continuity

---

1. Bukhari and Muslim.

of the self is innate, if he deeply thinks on the nature of his existence will find that he does not exist of his own self, nor are the means of the continuity of his self in his power. There is a being, self-existent, and living who created and sustains him. The Quran says: "There surely came over man a period of time when he was not a thing that could be spoken of. Surely We have created man from a small life germ uniting. We mean to try him, so We have made him hearing, seeing. Surely We have shown him the way, he may be thankful or unthankful." This contemplation will bear the fruit of love for God. For how could it be otherwise when man loves his own self which is dependent on Him, unless he be given up to the gratification of his passions and thereby forgetting his true self and his sustainer?

Secondly, if he thinks over the aim and scope of beneficence, he will find that no creature can show any purely disinterested favour to another because his motive will be either (1) praise or self-gratification for his generosity, or (2) hope of reward in the next world or divine

---

Quran LXXVI. 1-3.

pleasure.[1] Paradoxical though it sounds, deep insight into human nature leads us, inevitably, to the conclusion that man cannot be called "benefactor," inasmuch as his action is prompted by the idea of gain and barter. A true benefactor is one who in bestowing his favours has not the least idea of any sort of gain. Purely disinterested beneficence is the quality of the All-merciful Providence and hence He is the true object of love.

Thirdly, the appreciation of inward beauty, that is to say the contemplation of any attractive quality or qualities of the beloved, causes a stronger and more durable love than the passionate love of the flesh. However such a beloved will still be found lacking in beauty from the standpoint of perfection because the three genders are creatures and therefore cannot be called perfect. God alone is perfect Beauty, Holy, Independent, Omnipotent, All-Majesty, All-beneficent, All-merciful. With all this knowledge of His attributes we still do not know Him as He is. The Prophet says: "My praise of Thee cannot be comprehensive. Thou art such as wouldst

1. Ghazzali's remark should not be confounded with either egoistic or universalistic hedonism. See his remark on the affinity of souls.

praise Thyself." Are not these attributes sufficient to evoke love for Him? But beatitude is denied to the inwardly blind. They do not understand the attitude of the lovers of God towards Him. Jesus once passed by some ascetics who were reduced in body. "Why are you thus?" he said to them. And they replied, "Fear of hell and hope of heaven reduced us to this condition." "What a pity," rejoined Jesus, "your fear and hope is limited to creatures." Then he went onward and saw some more devotees, and put the same question. "We are devoted to God and revere Him for His love," they replied with downcast eyes. "Ye are the saints," exclaimed Jesus, "ye will have my company."[1]

Fourthly, the affinity between two souls meeting and loving each other is a mystery, but more mystery is the affinity between God and his loving devotee. It cannot, must not, be described before the uninitiated. Suffice it to say that the souls possessing the higher qualities of beneficence, sympathy, mercy, etc. have that affinity hinted at in the following saying of the Prophet: "Imitate divine attributes." For man has been created in the image of God, nay, he is, in a way, akin to Him. Says the Quran: "And when the Lord said

1. From uncanonical sayings of Christ.

to the angels: Suely I am going to create a mortal from dust, so when I have made him complete, and breathed into him of My Ruh (soul), fall down making obeisance to him." It is this affinity which is pointed out in the following tradition: God said to Moses, "I was sick and thou didst not visit Me." Moses replied, "O God, Thou art Lord of heaven and earth: how couldst Thou be sick?" God said, "A certain servant of Mine was sick: hadst thou visited him, thou wouldst have visited Me." Therefore our Prophet Muhammad has said: "Says God, My servant seeks to be near Me that I may make him My friend, and when I have made him My friend, I become his ear, his eye, his tongue."[2] It must, however, be remembered that mystical affinity vaguely conceived leads to extremes. Some have fallen into abject anthropomorphism; others have gone so far as to believe in the airy nothings of pantheism. These are all vagaries of the imagination, whether they take the form of "Ibn Allah," (son of God) or "Anal Haq" (I am God).

1. *Quran* XXXVIII. 71, 72.
2. See Bukhari *Hadis Qudsi.*
3. Al Ghazzali condemns all such expressions which are called by Cardinal Newman "eccentricities of the saints." He is

They are to a great extent responsible for the evils of superstition and scepticism.

These four causes, when properly understood, demonstrate that the true object of our love is God and therefore it has been enjoined: "Thou shalt love the Lord thy God with all thy heart and with all thy soul and with all thy mind."[1]

MAN'S HIGHEST HAPPINESS

The constitution of man possesses a number of powers and propensities, each of which has its own distinctive kind of enjoyment suited to it by nature. The appetite of hunger seeks food which preserves our body and the

---

aware of their liability to abuse and points out their error in a manner which six hundred years later took the form of Bishop Butler's dictum that reason cannot abdicate its right of judging obvious improprieties in religious doctrines and persons. "Ibn Allah" (son of God) refers to the orthodox Christian view of Jesus. "Anal Haq" (I am the truth, *i.e.* God) refers to the expression of Husain bin Mansur al Hallaj, who in 309 A.D. was crucified in Baghdad for his blasphemy. The Poet Hafiz says of him. "Jurmash an bud ki asrar huwaida mikard." (His crime was that he revealed the secrets)

1. *St. Matthew* XXII. 35-37. "And one of them, a lawyer, asked him a question, tempting him: Master, which is the great commandment in the law? And he said unto him: Thou shalt love the Lord thy God with all thy heart and with all thy soul, and with all thy mind." In the above passage the law referred to is *Deuteronomy* VI. 5, where instead of mind, the word might is used.

attainment of which is the delight of it, and so with every passion and propensity when their particular objects are attained. Similarly the moral faculty, call it inward sight, light of faith or reason—any name will do provided the object signified by it is rightly understood—delights in the attainment of its desideratum. I shall call it here the faculty of reason (not that wrangling reason of the scholastics and the dialecticians) —that distinctive quality which makes him lord of creation. This faculty delights in the possession of all possible knowledge. Even an expert in chess boastfully delights in the knowledge of the game, however insignificant it may be. And the higher the subject matter of our knowledge the greater our delight in it. For instance, we would take more pleasure in knowing the secrets of a king than the secrets of a vizier. Now delights are either (a) external, derived from the five senses, or (b) internal, such as love of superiority and power, love of the knowledge, etc., enjoyed by the mind. And the more the mind is noble the more there will be a desire for the second kind of delight. The simple will delight in dainty dishes, but a great mind leaving them aside will endanger his life and his honour and reputation from the jaws of death. Even sensuous delights present an amusing example of preference. An expert in chess while absorbed in playing will not come to his meals though hungry and repeatedly summoned, because the pleasure of checkmating his adversary is greater to him than the object of his appetite. Thus we see that inward delights, and they are chiefly love of knowledge and superiority, are preferred by noble minds. If then a man believes in a perfect Being, will not the pleasure of his contemplation be preferred by him and will it not absorb his whole self? Surely the delights of the righteous are indescribable for they are, even in this life, in a paradise which no eye has seen and no ear has heard.

Abu Sulaiman Darani,[1] the renowned Sufi, says: "There are servants of God whom neither fear of hell nor the hope of heaven can deviate from the divine love, how can the world with its temptations come in their way?" Abu Mahfuz Karkhi was once asked by his disciples: "Tell us what led you to devotion," but he kept quiet. "Is it the apprehension of death?" said one of them. "It matters little," replied the

1. Daran, a village near Damascus, where he died in 215 A.H.

saint. "Is it due to hell or to paradise?" inquired another. "What of them?" said the saint;" "both belong to a Supreme Being, if you love Him you will not be troubled by them." Saint Rabia[1] was once asked about her faith: "God forbid," answered Rabia, "if I serve him like a bad labourer thinking of his wages only." And then she sang: "Love draws me nigh, I know not why." Thus we see that the hearts of those who ate and drank and breathed like us felt delights of divine love which was their highest happiness.

If we think over man's gradual development we find that every stage of his life is followed by a new sort of delight. Children love playing and have no idea of the pleasures of courtship and marriage experienced by young men, who in their turn would not care to exchange their enjoyments for wealth and greatness which are the delights of the middle-aged men who consider all previous delights as insignificant and low. These last mentioned delights are also looked upon as unsubstantial and transitory by pure and noble souls fully developed.

---

1. A famous Muslim woman saint of Basrah, considered to be an authority on Sufiism. She died in 801 A.D.

The Quran says: "Know that this world's life is only sport and play and boasting among yourselves, and vying in the multiplication of wealth and children." "Say, shall I tell you what is better than these?" For the righteous are gardens with their Lord, beneath which rivers flow, to abide in them and pure mates and Allah's pleasure and Allah sees the servants." "Those who say: our Lord! surely we believe, so forgive us our faults, and keep us from the chastisement of fire; the patient and the truthful and the obedient and those who spend (benevolently) and those who ask forgiveness in morning times."[1]

Let us now point out some drawbacks which hinder the path of the divine love.

Man from his infancy is accustomed to enjoy sensual delights which are firmly implanted in him. Blind imitation of the creed with vague conception of the deity and his attributes fails to eradicate sensual delights and evoke the raptures of divine love. It is the dynamic force of direct contemplation of his attributes manifested in the universe that can prove an incentive for his love. To use a figure: a nation loves its national poet, but the feeling

1. *Quran* LVII. 20 and III. 14-16.

of one who studies the poet will be of exceeding strong love. The world is a masterpiece; he who studies it loves its Invisible Author in a manner which cannot be described but is felt by the favoured few. Another drawback which sounds like a paradox, should be deeply studied. It is as follows: when we find a person writing or doing any other work, the fact that he is living will be most apparent to us: that is to say, his life, knowledge, power and will, will be more apparent to us than his other internal qualities, *e.g.* colour, size etc. which being perceived by the eye may be doubted. Similarly stones, plants, animals, the earth, the sky, the stars, the elements, in fact everything in the universe reveals to us the knowledge, power and the will of its Originator Nay, the first and the foremost proof is our consciousness, because the knowledge that I exist is immediate,[1] and more apparent than our perceptions. Thus we see that man's actions are but one proof of his life, knowledge, power and will, but with reference to God the whole phenomenal existence with its law of causation and order and adaptability bears testimony of him and his

1. Compare Descartes : *Cogito ergo sum.*

attributes. Therefore, He is so dazzlingly apparent that the undetstanding of the people fails to see Him just as the bat which sees at night fails to see in daylight, because its imperfect sight cannot bear the light of the the sun, so our understanding is blurred by the effulgent light of His manifestations. The fact is that objects are known by their opposites but the conception of one who exists everywhere and who has no opposite would be most difficult. Besides, objects which differ in their respective significances can also be distinguished but if they have common significances the same difficulty will be felt. For instance, if the sun would have shone always without setting, we could have formed no idea of light, knowing simply that objects have certain colours. But the setting of the sun revealed to us the nature of light by comparing it with darkness. If then light, which is more perceptible and apparent, would have never been understood had there been no darkness notwithstanding its undeniable visibility, there is no wonder if God who is most apparent and all-pervading true light (Nur)[1]

1. Compare *Quran* XXIV. 35. "Allah is the light of the heavens and the earth : a likeness of His light is a pillar on which is a lamp, the lamp is in a glass (and) the glass is as it were a brightly shining star lit from a bleassed olive tree neither eastern

remains hidden, because if he would have disappeared (which means the annihilation of the universe), there would have been an idea of him by comparison as in the case of the light and darkness. Thus we see that the very mode of

---

nor western, the oil whereof almost gives light though fire touches it not (heads differ.) Allah guides to His light whom He pleases, and Allah sets forth parables for men and Allah is cognisant of all things." Al Ghazzali has written a separate treatise called *Mishkat ul Anwar* dealing exhaustively with the above passage. An excellent summary of his views is given by Razi in his Commentary, Vol. VI. 393-408. (Stamboul edition). In the above parable Islam is represented as a likeness of the divine light, a light placed high on a pillar so as to illumine the whole world, a light guarded by being placed in a glass so that no puff of wind can put it out, a light so resplendent that the glass itself in which it is placed is as a brilliant star. Just as a fig tree stands for a symbol of Judaism (see St. *Matthew* XXI. 19) the olive stands for Islam, which must give light to both the East and the West, and does not specifically belong to either one of them.

The doctrine of *Fana* is misunderstood by many Western scholars. Tennyson puts it:

"That each, who seems a separate whole
Should move his rounds and fusing all
The skirts of self again should fall
Remerging in the general soul.
Is faith as vague as all unsweet." (*In Memoriam* XLVII)

Ghazzali's vivid description is neither vague nor unsweet. To him *Fana* is " a prayer of rapturr." " In that state man is effaced from self, so that he is conscious neither of his body nor of outward things, nor of inward feelings. He is rapt from all these, journeying first to his Lord and then in his Lord, and if the thought that he is effaced from self occurs to him, that is a defect. The highest state is to be effaced from effacement." E. Whinfield: *Masnavi*, Introduction p. XXXVII.

his existence and manifestation is a drawback for human understanding. But he whose inward sight is keen and has strong intuition in his balanced state of mind neither sees nor knows any other active power save God omnipotent. Such a person neither sees the sky as the sky nor the earth as the earth—in fact sees nothing in the universe except in the light of its being work of an all-pervading True One. To use a figure : if a man looks at a poem or a writing, not as a collection of black lines scribbled on white sheets of paper but as a work of a poet or an author, he ought not to be considered as looking to anything other than the author. The universe is a unique masterpiece, a perfect song, he who reads it looks at the divine author and loves him. The true Mowahhid is one who sees nothing but God. He is not even aware of his self except as servant of God. Such a person will be called absorbed in Him ; he is effaced, the self is annihilated. These are facts known to him who sees intuitively, but weak minds do not know them. Even Ulama fail to express them adequately or consider the publicity of them as unsafe and unnecessary for the masses.

THE UNITY OF GOD*

THERE are four stages in the belief in the unity of God. The first is to utter the words: "There is no god but God" without experiencing any impression in the heart. This is the creed of the hypocrites. The second is to utter the above words and to believe that their meaning is also true. This is the dogma of ordinary Muslims. The third is to perceive by the inward light of the heart the truth of the above Kalima. Through the multiplicity of causes the mind arrives at the conception of the unity of the final cause. This is the stage of the initiates. The fourth is to gaze at the vision of an all-comprehensive, all-absorbing One, losing sight even of the duality of one's own self. This the highest stage of the true devotee. It is described by the Sufis as "Fanafittauhid" *i.e.* the effacement of one's individuality in contemplating the unity of God).[1] To use a simile these four stages

* *Ihya* IV. 5.

1. Usually *Fana* is translated as "annihilation," but Al Ghazzali here means what is implied in the statement: "To live, move, and have our being in Him."

may be compared with a walnut which is composed of an external hard rind, an internal skin, the kernel, and oil. The hard rind, which is bitter in taste, has no value except that it serves as a covering for some time. When the kernel is extracted the shell is thrown away. Similarly the hypocrite who, uttering the Kalima, is associated with the Muslims and safely enjoys their privileges, but at death is cut off from the faithful and falls headlong into perdition. The internal skin is more useful than the external inasmuch as it preserves the kernel and may be used, but is in no way equal to the kernel itself. Similarly the dogmatic belief of the ordinary Muslim is better than the lip service of the hypocrite, but lacks that broad clear insight which is described as " He whose heart Allah has opened to Islam walks in His light."

The kernel is undoubtedly the desired object, but it contains some substance which is removed when oil is being pressed out. Similarly the conception of an efficient final cause is the aim and object of the devotees, but is inferior to the vision of the all-pervading Holy One, because the conception of causality involves duality. But the objection may be urged: How can we ignore the diversities and multiplicities of the universe? Man has hands and feet, bones and blood, heart and soul, all distinct, yet he is one individual. When we are thinking of a dear old friend and suddenly he stands before us, we do not think of any multiplicity of his bodily organs, but are delighted to see him. The simile, though not quite appropriate is suggestive, especially for beginners. When they reach that stage they will themselves see its truth. Words fail to express the beatitude of that highest stage. It can be enjoyed, but not described.[1]

Let us consider the nature of the third stage. Man finds that God alone is the prime cause of everything. The world, its objects, life, death, happiness, misery, all have their source in His omnipotence. None is assciated with Him in this. When man comes to recognise this, he has no fear of anything, but puts his trust in God alone. But Satan tempts him by misrepresenting the agencies of the inorganic and organic worlds as potent factors independent in the shaping of his destiny.

---

1. "And thou shalt one day, if found worthy, be so defined. See thy God face to face, as thou dost now.'

Byron *Childe Harold's Pilgrimage.* CLV.

Think first of the inorganic world. Man thinks that crops depend on rain descending from clouds, and that clouds gather together owing to normal climatic conditions. Similarly his sailing on the sea depends on favourable winds. Without doubt, these are immediate causes, but they are not independent. Man who in the hour of need calls for God's mysterious help, forgets Him and turns to external causes as soon as he finds himself safe and sound. "So, when they ride in ships, they call upon Allah, being sincerely obedient to Him, but when He brings them safe to land, they associate others with Him. Thus they become ungrateful for what We have given them, so they might enjoy: but they shall soon know."[1] If a culprit, whose death sentence is revoked by the king, looks to the pen as his deliverer, will it not be sheer ignorance and ingratitude? Surely, the sun, the moon, the stars, the clouds, in fact, the whole universe is like a pen in the hand of an omnipotent dictator. When this kind of belief takes hold of the mind, Satan is disappointed in covertly tempting man, and uses subtle means, insinuating thus: "Do you not see that the

---

1. *Quran* XXIX. 65-66.

king has full power either to kill or favour you, and though the pen, in the above simile, is not your deliverer, the writer certainly is ?" As this sort of reflection led to the vexed question of free will, we have dealt with it already at some length.

At the outset, let us point out that just as an ant, owing to its limited sight, will see the point of the pen blackening a blank sheet of paper and not the fingers and hand of the writer, so the person whose mental sight is not keen will attribute the actions to the immediate doer only. But there are minds, which, with the searchlight of intuition, expose the lurking danger of wrongly attributing power to any except the All-powerful Omniscient Being. To them every atom in the universe speaks out truth of this revelation. They find tongues in trees, books in the running brooks, sermons in stones. The worldling will say : Though we have ears, we do not hear them. But asses also having ears do not hear. Verily there are such ears which hear words that have no sound, that are neither Arabic nor any other language, known to man. These words are drops in the boundless, unfathomable ocean of divine knowledge : "If the sea were ink for the words of my Lord, the sea would surely be consumed before the words of my Lord are exhausted."[1]

1, *Quran* XVIII. 109. Compare Jalal-ud-Din Rumi:
Air, earth, water, and fire are God's servants.
To us they seem lifeless, but to God living.
In God's presence fire ever waits to do its service.
Like a submissive lover with no will of its own.
When you strike steel on flint fire leaps forth;
But 'tis by God's command it thus steps forth;
Strike not together the flint and steel of wrong,
For the pair will generate more, like man and woman.
The flint and steel are themselves causes, yet
Look higher for the First Cause, O righteous man!
For that Cause precedes this second cause.
How can a cause exist of itself without precedent cause?
That Cause makes this cause operative,
And again helpless and inoperative.
That Cause, which is a guiding light to the prophets,
That, I say, is higher than these second causes,
Man's minds recognise these second causes,
But only prophets perceive the action of the First Cause

E. Whinfield: *Masnavi*, 2nd ed. 1898, p. 16

THE LOVE OF GOD AND ITS SIGNS*

LOVE of God is the highest stage of our soul's progress and her *summum bonum.* Repentance, patience, piety, and other virtues are all preliminary steps. Although rare, these qualities are found in true devotees and the commonality, though devoid of them, at any rate believe in them. Love of God is not only very rare : the possibility of it is doubted, even by some Ulama who call it simply service. For, in their opinion, love exists amongst species of the same kind, but God being ultra-mundane and not of our kind, His love is an impossibility and hence the much talked of ecstatic states of the "true lovers of God" are mere delusions. As this is far from truth and impedes the progress of the soul, by spreading false notions, we shall briefly discuss the subject. First we shall quote passages from the Quran and the Hadith testifying to the existence of the love of God.

"O you who believe, whosoever from among you turns back from his religion, then

---

* *Ihya* IV. 6.

Allah will bring a people : He shall love them, and they shall love Him, lowly before the believers, mightily against the unbelievers, they shall strive hard in Allah's way and shall not fear the censure of any censurer : this is Allah's grace, He gives it to whom He pleases and Allah is ample-giving, knowing."[1]

"And there are some among men who take for themselves objects of worship besides Allah, whom they love. Allah and those who believe are stronger in love of Allah."[2] These passages not only refer to the existence of the love of God but point to the difference in degree. The Prophet has taught us that the love of God is one of the conditions of faith. "None among you shall be a believer until he loves Allah and His Apostle more than anything else."[3]

True, as the Quran says, "if your fathers and your sons and your brethren and your mates and your kinsfolk and property which you have acquired and trade the dullness of which you fear, and dwellings which you like, are dearer to you than Allah and His Apostle and striving in

---

1. *Quran* V. 54.
2. *Quran* II. 165.
3. Bukhari and Muslim.

His way, then wait till Allah brings about His command, and Allah does not guide the transgressing people."[1]

A man came to the Prophet and said: "I love thee, O Apostle of God." "Be ready for poverty," replied the Prophet. "And I love Allah," said the man. "Prepare to face tribulations,"[2] replied the Prophet. The following tradition is narrated by the Khalif Omar: The Prophet one day saw Musab, son of Umair, coming to him with a lambskin round his loins. "Look," said the Prophet to his companions, "how God has illumined his heart. I have seen him living in ease and well provided by his parents but now the love of Allah and His Apostle has wrought a change in him."[3]

The Prophet used to pray thus: "My God! give me Thy love and the love of him who loves Thee and the love of that action which will bring me nearer to Thee and make Thy love sweeter than cold water to the thirsty."[4]

"Verily Allah loves those who repent and

---

1. *Quran* IX. 24.
2. Tirmizi.
3. Abu Naim.
4. Tirmizi.

those who purify themselves."[1] Say, "If you love Allah, then follow me. Allah will love you and forgive you your faults, and Allah is Forgiving, Merciful."[2] We have said before that love means yearning towards a desired object and that beneficence and beauty, whether perceived or conceived, equally attract our hearts. But in using the word love for God, no such meaning is possible as it implies imperfection. God's love towards men is the love of His own work. Someone read the following verse of the Quran: "He loves them and they love him" in front of Shaikh Abu Said of Mohanna, who interpreted it saying: "He loves Himself because He alone exists. Surely an author who likes himself, his love is limited to his self. God's love means lifting the veil from the heart of His servant, so that he might gaze at Him. It also means drawing him closer to Himself. Let us give an illustration. A king permits some of his slaves to approach his pre-

1. *Quran* II. 222. Repentance is the first step towards God. Comp. *St. Matthew* III. 2.

2. *Quran* III. 30. Keeping God's commandments revealed through His holy prophets constitutes love of Him. Comp. St. *John*. XV. 10: "If ye keep my commandments ye shall abide in my love; even as I keep my Father's commandments and abide in His love."

sence, not because he requires them but because the slaves possess or are acquiring certain qualities which are worthy of being displayed before the royal presence. This privilege, this lifting of the veil, brings us nearer to the conception of God's love. But it must be remembered that approaching the divine presence should entirely exclude the idea of space, for then it would imply change in Him, which is absurd. Divine proximity means the attainment of Godly virtues by abstaining from the promptings of the flesh and hence it implies approach from the point of view of quality and not of space. For example, two persons meet together either when both of them proceed towards each other or one is stationary and the other starts and approaches him. Again a pupil strives to come up to the level of his teacher's knowledge, who is resting in his elevated position. His uphill journey towards knowledge keeps him restless and he climbs higher and higher till he catches a glimpse of the halo which surrounds his master's countenance. The nature of divine proximity resembles this inward journey of the pupil ; that is, the more a man acquires insight into the nature of things, and by subjugating his passions leads the life of righteousness, the nearer will he be coming to his Lord. But it must be remembered that a pupil may equal his teacher, even be greater than he, but as regards divine proximity, no such equality is possible. God's love means that which purifies the heart of His servant in a manner that he may be worthy of being admitted before His holy Presence.

It may be asked : " How can we know that God loves a certain person ?" My answer is that there are signs which bear testimony to it. The Prophet says : When God loves His servant, He sends tribulations, and when He loves him most he severs his connection from everything. Someone said to Jesus : " Why do you not buy a mule for yourself "? Jesus answered : " My God will not tolerate that I should concern myself with a mule." Another saying of Muhammad is reported thus : When God loves any of His servants He sends tribulations. If he patiently bears them, he is favoured, and if he cheerfully faces them, he is singled out as chosen of God. Surely it is this joyous attitude of his mind, whether evil befalls him or good, that is the chief sign of love. Such minds are providentially taken care of in their thoughts and deeds and in all their dealings with men. The veil is lifted and they live in wrapped communion.

As for the signs of a man's love for God, let it be borne in mind that everybody claims His love, but few really love Him. Beware of self-deception; verify your statement by introspection. Love is like a tree rooted in the ground ending its shoots above the starry heaven; its fruit is found in the heart, the tongue and the limbs of the lover—in fact, his whole self is a witness to love just as smoke is a sure sign of fire burning.

Let us, then, trace the signs which are found in the true lover.

Death is a pleasure to him, for it removes the barrier of body and lets the fluttering soul free to soar and sing in the blissful abode of his beloved. Sufyan Thauri used to say: "He who doubts dislikes death, because a friend will never dislike meeting a friend."[1]

A certain Sufi asked a hermit whether he wished for death, but he gave no answer. Then the Sufi said to him: "Had you been a true hermit you would have liked

1. A Sufi of great renown: died at Baghdad in 840 A.D.

death. The Quran says: If the future abode with Allah is especially for you to the exclusion of the people, then invoke death if you are truthful. They will never wish it on account of what their hands have sent on before, and Allah knows the unjust."[1] The hermit replied: "But the Prophet says: Do not wish for death." "Then you are suffering," said the Sufi, "because acquiescence in divine decree is better than trying to escape it."

It may be asked here: Can he who does not like death be God's lover? Let us consider first the nature of his dislike. It is due to his attachment to the worldly objects, wife, children, and so forth, but it is possible that with this attachment, which no doubt comes in the way of his love of God, there may be some inclination towards His love, because there are degrees of His love. Or it may be that his dislike is due to his feeling of unpreparedness in the path of love. He would like to love more so that he might be able to purify himself just as a lover hearing of his beloved's arrival would like to be given some time for making preparations for a fitting reception. For these reasons if a devotee

1. *Quran* II. 94-95.

dislikes death, he can still be His lover, though of inferior type.

He should prefer, both inwardly and outwardly God's pleasure to his desires. For he who follows the dictates of his desires is no true lover, for the true lover's will is his beloved's. But human nature is so constituted that such selfless beings are very rare. Patients would like to be cured but they often eat things which are injurious to their health. Similarly, a person would like to love God but very often follows his own impulses. Noman was a sinner, who being repeatedly excused by the Prophet was at last flogged. While he was being flogged a certain person cursed him for his iniquity. " Do not curse him," said he ; " he has a regard for God and His Apostle."

Experience tells us that he who loves, loves the things connected with his beloved. Therefore another sure sign of God's love is the love of His creatures who are created by and are dependent on him ; for he who loves an author or poet, will he not love his work or poem ? But this stage is reached when the lover's heart is immersed in love and the more he is absorbed in Him, the more will he love His creatures, so much so that even the objects which hurt him will not be disliked by him—in fact the problem of evil is transcended in his love for Him.

It may be objected here that it follows that he loves the evil-doers and sinners. But a deep insight into the nature of such love shows that he loves them as creatures of God, but at the same time hates their actions which are contrary to the command of his Beloved. If this point is lost sight of, people are apt to be misguided in their love or hatred of His creatures. If they show their love towards any sinner, let it be in pure compassion, and not any sense of taking the sin lightly. Similarly their hatred should proceed from the consciousness of His stern law and justice and not from ruthless bigotry.

In one of the Hadis Qudsi[1] God has said: " My saints are those who cry like a child for My love, who remember Me like a fearless lion at the sight of iniquities."

A reverent attitude of mind is another sign of his love. Some hold that fear is opposed to love, but the truth is that just as the con-

1. Hadis Qudsi is that kind of tradition in which God is Himself reported to speak.

ception of beauty generates love, the knowledge of His sublime majesty produces the feeling of awe in us. Lovers meet with fears which are unknown to others.[1] There is the fear of being disregarded. There is fear of the veil being drawn down. There is the fear of their being turned away. When the Sura Hud was revealed, in which the awful doom of the wicked nations is narrated: "Away with Samood, away with Midian," the Prophet heaved a sigh and said: "This Sura has turned me into an old man." He who loves His nearness will feel acutely the fear of being thrown way from Him. There is another fear of remaining at a particular stage and not rising higher, for the ascending degrees of His nearness are infinite. A true lover is always trying to draw nearer and nearer to Him. "A thin veil covers my heart," says the Prophet, "then I ask for His forgiveness seventy times in

---

1. Comp:

"Let knowledge grow from more to more,
But more of reverence in us dwell;
Than mind and soul, according well.
May make one music as before,
But vaster. We are fools and slight;
We mock Thee when we do not fear;
But help Thy foolish ones to bear
Help Thy vain worlds to bear Thy light.

Tennyson.

day and night."[1] This means that the Prophet was always ascending the scales of His nearness, asking for His forgiveness at every stage which was found lower than the next one.

There is another fear of over-confidence which slackens the efforts and mars progress. Hope with fear should be the guide of love. Some Sufis say that he who worships God without fear is liable to err and fall ; he who worships Him with fear turns gloomy and is cast off, but he who lovingly worships Him with hope and fear is admitted by Him and favoured. Therefore lovers should fear Him and those who fear Him should love Him. Even excess of His love contains an inkling of fear : it is like salt in food. For human nature cannot bear the white heat of His love, if it is not chastened and tempered by the fear of the Lord.

Keeping love secret and giving no publicity to it is another sign of His love. For love is the beloved's secret : it should not be revealed nor openly professed. However, if he is over-powered by the force of his love, and unwittingly and without the least dissimulation his secret is out, he is not to be blamed. Some Sufis say : He

---

1. See Bukhari.

who is very often pointing towards Him is far from Him, because he feigns and makes a show of his love of Him. Zunnun[1] of Egypt once went to pay a visit to one of his brother Sufis, who was in distress, and who used to talk of his love openly. "He who feels the severity of pain inflicted by Him," said Zunnun, "is no lover." "He who finds no pleasure in such pain," returned the Sufi, "is no lover." "True," replied Zunnun, "but I say to you that he who trumpets his love of Him is no lover." The Sufi felt the force of Zunnun's words and fell down prostrate before God and repented and did not talk again of his love.

It may be objected: Divine love is the highest stage, it would be better to manifest it, where is the harm? No doubt love is good and if of itself it is evident, there is no harm, but those who give themselves trouble to make it known are blamable. Let our hearts speak, let our deeds proclaim it, but not our tongues. Nay, he should always aim at making it evident before his Beloved. The gospel says: "Take heed that ye do not give your alms before men to be seen: otherwise ye have no reward of your

1. Called the "father of Sufiism." He founded a sect of Sufis in Egypt. He died in 860 A.D.

Father which is in heavens. Therefore, when thou dost thine alms do not sound a trumpet before thee as the hypocrites do in the synagogues and in the streets, that they may have the glory of men. Verily I say unto you they have their reward. But when thou dost alms let not thy left hand know what thy right hand doth. That thine alms may be in secret, and thy Father which seeth in secret Himself shall reward thee openly. Moreover, when ye fast, be not as the hypocrites, of sad countenance : for they disfigure their faces, that they may appear unto men to fast. Verily I say unto you they have their reward. But thou, when thou fastest, anoint thine head and wash thy face, that thou appear not unto men to fast, but unto thy Father which is in secret; and thy Father which seeth in secret shall reward thee openly."[1]

The essence of religion is love; some signs of which have been enumerated above. The love of God may be of two kinds. Some love Him for His bounties, others for His perfect beauty irrespective of bounties. The former love increases according to the bounties received, but the latter love is the direct result of the

---

1. St. *Matthew* VI. 17 1-4; 16-18.

contemplation of His perfect attributes and is constant even in tribulations. "These are His favoured few," says Junaid of Baghdad.[1] But there are many who pose as his lovers and with much talk of his love lack the signs of true love. They are deluded by the devil, slaves of their passions, seeking a hollow reputation, shameless hypocrites who try to deceive the Omniscient Lord their Creator. They are all enemies of God, whether they are revered as divines or Sufis. Sahl of Taster who used to address everyone as "friend," was once asked by a person the reason of his doing so, as all men could not be his friends. Sahl whispered in his ear saying: "He will either be a believer or a hypocrite; if he is a believer, he is God's friend; if a hypocrite, the devil's friend."

Abu Turab Nakshabi has composed some verses describing the signs of love. Their translation is as follows:

Do not profess your love. Hearken to me: These are the signs of his love. The bitterness of tribulations is sweet to him, he is happy for he believes that everything proceeds from Him; for praise or censure he cares not,

1. A celebrated Sufi called Syed Uttaifa (chief of the sect.) He died at Baghdad in 911 A.D.

the will of his beloved is his will. While his heart is burning with love his countenance is radiant with joy. He guards the secret of love with all his might, and no thought save of his beloved enters into his mind. Yahya bin Maaz Razi[1] adds some lines: "Another sign is that he is up and ready like a diver at the bank of a river; he sighs and sheds tears in the gloom of night, and day and night he appears as if fighting for the sacred cause of his love. He entrusts his whole self to his love and gladly acquiescing abides in his love.[2]

---

1. A theologian and Sufi of Ray in Persia. He died in 871 A.D.

2. Comp.

Good shepherd, tell this youth what it's to love:
It is to be all made of sighs and tears;
It is to be all made of faith and service;
It is to be all made of fantasy,
All made of passion and all made of wishes;
All adoration, duty, and observance,
All humbleness, all patience and impatience,
All purity, all trial, all observance.

Shakespeare: As You Like It: *Act* V.

" RIZA " OR JOYOUS SUBMISSION TO HIS WILL*

RIZA is the quintessence of love and is one of the highest stages of the favoured few. But some doubt its existence, saying, how can man be joyous for what is against his own will? He may submit to God's will, but it does not follow that he also shares the feeling of joy. We shall discuss the nature of Riza and prove its existence.

Let us first turn to the Quarn and the Hadis. " Allah has promised to the believing men and the believing women gardens, beneath which rivers flow, to abide in them, and goodly dwellings in gardens of perpetual abode and best of all is Allah's goodly pleasure that is the grand achievement."[1] In this passage God's pleasure (Rizwan) is described as best of all blessings. In another passage this blessing is also bestowed on those who joyfully submit to His will. " Allah is well pleased with them and they are well pleased with Him ; that is for him who fears

---

* *Ihya* IV. 6.

1. *Quran* IX. 72.

his Lord."[1] Who fear the beneficent God in secret and come with a penitent heart, enter it in peace that is the day of abiding. They have therein what they wish *and with Us is more yet.*" Some commentators while commenting on the words in italics say that three gifts will be given in Paradise: (i) a rare gift of which "no soul knows (in this world) what is hidden for them of that which will refresh the eyes."[2] (ii) The salutation as mentioned in the Quran: "Peace (Salam) a word from the merciful Lord."[3] (iii) His goodly grace and pleasure as mentioned in "wa Rizwanumminallahi akbar" (and best of all is Allah's goodly pleasure).

The Prophet once asked some of his companions to point out the signs of the faith which they professed. "O Apostle of God," said the companions, "we are patient in tribulations, grateful in felicity and pleased with what is ordained." "Ye are Muslims," said the Prophet. Again the Prophet said: "Ye who are poor be pleased with what God has put you in and then you shall have your reward."

---

1. *Quran* XCVIII. 8.
2. *Quran* XXXII. 17.
3. *Quran* XXXVI. 58

Let us discuss the nature of Riza. Those who deny the existence of Riza, saying that man can be patient in sufferings but joyous submission to His will is not possible, really deny the existence of love and its all-absorbing nature. A lover always loves his beloved's actions. Now this love of actions is of two kinds : (1) Redemption from the experience of pain caused by mental or physical suffering.

Experience shows that many warriors while enraged do not feel the pain of their wounds, and know it only when they see blood gushing from them. Even when man is engaged in some action which absorbs his attention, the pain of a thorn pricking him will not be felt. If then in such cases, and there are many such, pain is not felt, will it not be possible that a devotee who is absorbed in Him does not feel pain, which in his belief is inflicted by his Beloved ?

Or (2) although pain is felt, he would desire it just as a patient who feels the pain caused by the surgeon's lancet is glad to be operated upon and is pleased with the surgeon's action. Similarly he who firmly believes that tribulations are like God-send curatives will be pleased with them and be thankful to God. Anyone who ponders over the nature of the above mentioned kinds and then in the light of them reads the lives and the sayings of the lovers of God, will, I believe, be convinced of the existence of Riza.

Saint Basher, son of Harith, narrated the story : In the Sharkia Lane of Baghdad I saw a man who received a thousand stripes, but did not cry in his agony. He was then sent to prison and I followed him. " Why have you been punished so mercilessly ? " I asked. " Because they have found out the secret of my love." " But why were you so strangely quiet while you were punished so severely?" I asked in astonishment. " Because," answered the poor fellow with a sigh, " she was looking at me from her balcony." " Oh! that you might see the true Beloved," I murmurred. Hearing this, his colour at once changed ; and with a loud cry he fell dead.

The same saint tells another story : " While I was a student of Sufiism I went to Jazirai Abbadan,[1] where I saw a blind epileptic leper, lying on the ground while worms were eating his flesh. I sat by his side and placed

1. In Tigris.

his head on my lap and spoke gently to him. When he came to his senses, he spoke: 'Who is this stranger who comes between me and my Lord? Even if each and every limb is severed from my body, I will love Him.' That scene of Riza, says the saint, I shall never forget; it is a life-long lesson for me."

It is said that Christ once saw a blind, forlorn leper who was praying: "Blessed art Thou, O Lord! who hast saved me from such maladies which have overtaken many of us." "Art thou not in misery?" asked Christ. "Tell me which is that malady which has not overtaken thee." "Thank God," cried the leper, "I am not like him who does not know God." "You are right," said Christ. "Give me your hand." And the breath of Christ instantly healed the leper, and he became one of his followers.

The Prophet's companion Said bin Wakas[1] lost his eyesight in old age, and resigning his post returned to Mecca. People flocked to him for blessing as he was known to be one whose prayers were always heard. Says Abdullah bin Said: "I was then a mere boy; I too went to pay my respects to the venerable Said. He

1 He conquered Persia in the time of Khalifa Omar.

spake kindly to me and blessed me. Then I said: 'Said, uncle,[1] how is it that you who are praying for everybody but would not pray for the restoration of your eyesight?' 'My son,' answered Said with a smile, 'to be pleased with His sweet will is better than eyesight."

Some people went to see Shibli at a lunatic asylum where he was imprisoned. "Who are you?" asked the saint. "Friends," they all replied with one voice. Hearing this Shibli fetched some stones and began to pelt at them, and they all fled calling him a madman. "What's this?" exclaimed Shibli. "You call yourselves my friends but if you are sincere, bear patiently what ye receive from me," and then he sang: "His love has turned my brain. Have you ever seen a lover who is not intoxicated with love?"

These narratives point out that Riza or joyous submission to God's will is possible and is one of the highest stages to which the souls of true devotees could aspire. People believe in eccentricities of Cupid's votaries but give no ear to the ecstasies of the true lovers of God. Perhaps they have no eyes to look at the manifestation of His beauty; no ears to listen to the

1. The Arabs address elders in this way.

music of His love, no heart to gaze at and enjoy His sweet presence. Perhaps they are proud of their learning and think too much of their good deeds but they have no idea of humble and broken hearts.

A certain nobleman of Bustam, comely in appearance and lordly in bearing, used to attend the sermons of saint Bayazid of Bustam.[1] One day he said to the saint: "For thirty years I have been keeping fasts, waking for the whole night and offering my prayers, but still I do not find in me the animating force of what you teach although I believe in it and cherish love for you." "Thirty years?" ejaculated the saint: "Why, for three hundred years if you do as you have done till now, you will not have a bit of it." "How is that?" asked the astonished nobleman. "Because," answered the saint, "the veil of your egotism has fallen heavily on your mind's eye." The chief then asked the saint to tell him of some remedy, but he declined saying that the chief would not like to take it. "But do tell me," entreated the nobleman. "And I will try my best to follow your kind

1. One or the most renowned of the early Sufis. His grandfather was a Magian who accepted Islam. He was born in 777 A.D. and died at a great age in 878 A.D.

advice." "Listen then," calmly answered the saint, "this very moment go to the barber, get your head and beard shaved, take off this apparel, and gird your loins with a piece of blanket; gather children round you and tell them that whosoever gives you a slap with the hand will get a walnut, pass through the throngs in all the bazars, followed by those children and then show yourself to your intimate friends."

"Subhan Allāh!" exclaimed the chief. "Do you say that to me?" "Hold thy tongue," retorted the saint; 'thy Subhan Allah is blasphemy'!" "How is that?" asked the chief. "Because," replied the saint, "you uttered Subhan Allah not for any reverence for the Holy Being but out of respect for your own vain self." "Well," said the chief, "tell me some other remedy, please." "Try this remedy first," continued the saint. "I cannot do so," rejoined the chief. "There you are," spoke the saint calmly. "Did I not tell you that you would not like the remedy?"

Our egoistic tendencies impede the progress of our souls towards higher virtues, and hence some of us go the length of denying the possibility of their existence. Let the lives of the true lovers of God be our guide!

THE SEVEN VALLEYS

KNOW, my brethren, that worship is the fruit of knowledge, the benefit of life and the capital of virtuous. It is the aim and object of men of noble aspirations having keen inward sight. It is their *summum bonum* and their everlasting Paradise. "I am your Creator," says the Quran. "Worship Me. You will have your recompense and your efforts will be rewarded."

Worship then is essential for man but it is beset with difficulties and hardships. It has stumbling blocks and pitfalls in its tortuous path which is haunted by cut-throats and goblins while helpers are scarce and friends are few. But this path of worship must be dangerous, for says the Prophet, "Paradise is surrounded by sufferings and covered by tribulations, while Hell abounds in ease and free enjoyment of passions. Poor man! he is weak, his engagements are heavy: times are hard and life is short. But journey from here to hereafter being unavoidable, if he neglects taking necessary provisions he is sure to perish. Ponder over the gravity of the situation and the seriousness of our condition. By Allah our lot is pitiable indeed, for many are called but few are chosen.

When I found the path of worship so difficult and dangerous I composed certain works, chiefly *Ihya ulum-iddin* in which I pointed out the ways and means of surmounting those difficulties, facing the dangers boldly and crossing the path with success. But certain persons looking to the outward expressions of my work failed to understand the meaning and purpose of it and not only rejected the book* but treated it in a manner unbecoming of a Muslim. But I was not disheartened for these were persons who used to ridicule the Holy Quran calling it "The Stories of the Ancients." Nor was I offended for I felt pity on them for they knew not what they were doing to themselves. I hate disputations now but I must do something for them. So out of compassion for my brethren I prayed to God to enlighten me on the subject in a new manner.

*During the life time of the author the book was publicly burnt in the market bv the Ulama of Spain, the land of Inquisition.

Listen, then, that the first requisite which awakens man from the lethargy of forgetfulness and turns him towards the path, is God's grace which stirs the mind to meditate thus :—

I am the recipient of so many gifts—life, power, reason, speech—and I find myself mysteriously protected from many troubles and evils. Who is my benefactor? who is my saviour? I must be grateful to him in a fitting manner otherwise the gifts will be taken away and I shall be undone. These gifts reveal their purpose like tools in the hands of an artisan and the world appears to me like a beautiful picture leading my thoughts towards the painter.

The soliloquy takes him to the Valley of

The Valley of Knowledge.

Knowledge where implicit faith in the Divine Messenger leads the way and tells him :—

The Benefactor is that One Being who has no associate with Him. He is thy Creator who is Omnipresent though unseen, whose Commandments must be obeyed both inwardly and outwardly. He has so ordained that the good shall be rewarded and the wicked punished. The choice is now thine for thou art held responsible for thy actions. Acquire knowledge under God-fearing *Ulama* with a conviction that knows no wavering.

When the Valley of Knowledge is crossed man prepares for worship, but his guilty conscience upbraids him saying, "Canst thou knock at the door of the Sanctuary? Away with thy pollutious abominations!"

The Valley of Repentance

The poor sinner falls down in the Valley of Repentance when a voice is heard, "Repent, repent! for thy Lord is Forgiving. He now takes heart and rising with joy proceeds further.

The Valley of Stumbling blocks.

And he enters into a Valley full of Stumbling blocks chief of which are four in number, *viz.*, the tempting world; the attracting people; the old enemy Satan and the inordinate self. Let him have four counterforces so as to tide over the difficulty. Try to choose retired life; avoid mixing with all sorts of people; fight out the old enemy and control thyself by the bridle of piety.

Let it be remembered that the fourfold counterforces have to face four other psychological troubles, *viz.*, (1) Anxious care about man's daily bread as a result of his retirement. (2)

Doubts and anxieties about his private affairs disturbing peace of his mind. (3) Worries, hardships and indignities for want of social contact. For when man wishes to serve his God, Satan attacks him openly and secretly from all sides. (4) Unpleasant happenings and unexpected sufferings as the outcome of his destiny.

The Valley of Tribulations.

These psychological troubles throw the poor worshipper into the Valley of Tribulations. In this plight let man protect himself by (1) Dependence on God in the matter of his sustenance. (2) Invocation of His help when he finds himself helpless. (3) Patience in sufferings. (4) Joyous submission to His Will.

Crossing this fearful Valley of Tribulations man thinks that the passage will not be easy but to his amazement he finds that service is uninteresting, prayers are mechanical and contemplation has no pleasure. He is indolent, melancholy and stupid. Puzzled and perplexed he now enters into the Thundering Valley. The lightning flash of Hope dazzles his sight and he falls down trembling when he hears the deafening sound of the thunder of Fear. His eyes brimming with tears imitate the

The Thundering Valley.

clouds and his pure thoughts flash with the lightning. In a moment the mystery of Human Responsibility with its reward for good actions and punishment for wicked deeds was solved. Henceforth his worship will not be lip service and his daily work will not be a drudgery. Soaring on high he will ply on the wings of Hope and Fear. With a light heart, in a happy mood, he was now proceeding further when suddenly the Abysmal Valley presents its dreadful sight. Looking deep into the nature of his actions he found that those who were good were either actuated by the desire of winning the approbation of his fellow men or were simply the outcome of vainglory. On one side he saw the hydra-headed monster[1] of hypocrisy lurking and on the other side the bewitching Pandora of Conceit with her box open.[2] In despair he knew not what to do when, lo! the Angel of Sincerity emerged from the depth of his heart and taking him by the arm carried him through the valley.

The Abysmal Valley.

Expressing his gratitude for the Divine

1. The old Greeks' water-serpent with many heads which when cut off were succeeded by others.

2. In Greek mythology a beautiful woman to whom Jupiter gave a box containing all the ills of human life, which, on the box being opened, spread over all the earth.

favour he was proceeding further when the thought of multifarious favours for his unworthy self and his incapacity to do full justice to his thanksgivings overwhelmed him.

The Valley of Hymns.

This was the Valley of Hymns where, mortal as he was, he tried his best to sing the songs of praise to the Immortal Being. The Invisible Hand of Divine Mercy then opened the door of the Garden of Love, he was ushered in with body and soul for both had played their part directly and indirectly. Here ends the journey. The worshipper is now living among his fellow men like traveller but his heart lives in Him waiting to carry out the last order, " O soul that art at peace ! return to thy Creator well-pleased, well pleasing. Then enter among My Servants and enter into My Paradise. (Quran ch. LXXXIX al-Fajr).

INDEX